THREE
CHRISTIAN
CAPITALS

UNA'S LECTURES

Una's Lectures, delivered annually on the Berkeley campus, memorialize Una Smith, who received her B.S. in History from Berkeley in 1911 and her M.A. in 1913. They express her esteem for the humanities in enlarging the scope of the individual mind. When appropriate, books deriving from the Una's Lectureship are published by the University of California Press:

The Resources of Kind: Genre-Theory in the Renaissance,
by Rosalie L. Colie. 1973
From the Poetry of Sumer: Creation, Glorification, Adoration,
by Samuel Noah Kramer. 1979
The Making of Elizabethan Foreign Policy, 1558–1603,
by R. B. Wernham. 1980
Three Christian Capitals: Topography and Politics,
by Richard Krautheimer. 1982

THREE
CHRISTIAN
CAPITALS

TOPOGRAPHY AND POLITICS

Richard Krautheimer

UNIVERSITY OF CALIFORNIA PRESS
Berkeley • Los Angeles • London

University of California Press
Berkeley and Los Angeles, California

University of California Press, Ltd.
London, England

© 1983 by
The Regents of the University of California
Printed in the United States of America
1   2   3   4   5   6   7   8   9

*Library of Congress Cataloging in Publication
Data*
Krautheimer, Richard, 1897–
  Three Christian capitals.

  (Una's lectures ; 4)
  Four rev. and enl. lectures originally given at
the University of Calif., Berkeley, in May 1979.
  Includes bibliographical references and index.
  1. Rome (Italy)–Description–Addresses, essays, lectures.   2. Istanbul (Turkey)–Description–Addresses, essays, lectures.   3. Milan
(Italy)–Description–Addresses, essays, lectures.
4. Christian antiquities–Italy–Rome–Addresses, essays, lectures.   5. Christian antiquities–Turkey–Istanbul–Addresses, essays,
lectures.   6. Christian antiquities–Italy–Milan–
Addresses, essays, lectures.   7. Church history–
Primitive and early church, ca. 30–600–Addresses, essays, lectures.   I. Title.   II. Series.
DG63.K7   937'.08   81-13148
ISBN 0-520-04541-6 AACR2

The publication of this book has been supported
by a generous grant from the Una Lecture Committee of the University of California, Berkeley.

Contents

List of Illustrations

For sources of illustrations, the following abbreviations are used:

AFMV Archivio Fotografico Musei Vaticani, Vatican City
FU Fototeca Unione, American Academy, Rome
DAI Deutsches Archäologisches Institut, Rome and Istanbul
PCAS Pontificia Commissione di Archeologia Sacra, Rome
SAL Soprintendenza Archeologica di Lombardia, Milan

For books, the abbreviations used are given in the list of frequently cited works.

Preface

The four lectures included in this book in revised and slightly enlarged form were delivered at the University of California, Berkeley, in May 1979 in memory of Una Smith Ross, a graduate of the university, class of 1901. I am deeply indebted to Mr. Hunter Ross, her husband, who has generously funded the series of Una Lectures to be given annually; to the members of the committee, headed by Professor Thomas G. Barnes, for the hospitality extended to my wife and myself in their homes as well as at the faculty club; and to the faculty and students who attended the lectures and received them, I feel, without disapproval. Among the faculty my particular thanks are due to Professors Peter Brown, Gerard E. Caspary, and David Wright for valuable suggestions proffered in many friendly talks.

The lectures represent an experiment. They are the attempt of an old historian of art to explore the borders of his field and to transgress into that of political history: to view the architectural monuments of the Christian capitals of the fourth and fifth centuries and their location within the urban texture as reflecting the political realities and ideologies of Constantinian Rome, Constantinople, Milan, and early papal Rome. Whether I have succeeded in achieving this aim I must leave to the reader, but I hope at least to have stimulated further research along lines which I deem important.

Originally I had hoped to be able to deal in a fifth chapter with one more Christian capital—Trier—where since 1943 excavations have brought to light remains of the imperial palace and of a huge twin cathedral. A thorough study of the material published so far and a correspondence with Dr. Theodor K. Kempf, who is in charge of the work at Trier, have convinced me that an attempt at summing up the results of the excavation before the publication of the final report would be premature.

Thus, much as I regret it, I must resign myself to omitting Trier. Hence, this book will have to remain *Three Christian Capitals*.

For help in preparing the lectures and the present final version, I am equally indebted to my assistant of many years, Joan Barclay Lloyd, at present of Latrobe University, Melbourne. Her clever hand also supplied both the maps and the reconstruction drawings of S. Giovanni in Laterano and of the interior of Sto. Stefano Rotondo in Rome, as well as adjusting a number of other drawings. Mrs. Elizabeth Schwartzbaum and Miss June Taboroff undertook the task of deciphering my handwriting and typing the manuscript. Mrs. Marilyn Schwartz of the University of California Press and Miss Helen Tartar as editors saw the manuscript through press. Mrs. Cothran W. Ceen, finally, was good enough to share with me the tedious and ever so necessary task of proofreading. My warm thanks go to all of them.

Rome, September 1980

Introduction

Topography, so say the dictionaries, is a scholarly discipline given over to the description or the discovery of a particular locality and the location within it of specific sites. It thus identifies a structure or its remains or simply the place it once occupied with a building known from historical sources to have risen in that neighborhood: a set of walls mentioned by ancient writers as having been located on the Roman Forum at the foot of the Palatine turns out to have been the compound of the Vestals; the ruins of a large basilica on another part of the Forum are revealed by a number of passages in Livy, Tacitus, and other Roman historians as those of the Basilica Aemilia, founded in 179 B.C. by the consul Marcus Aemilius Lepidus and his colleague; or, closer to home, Wall Street is easily identified through old maps and archeological finds as the site of the early city wall of New York. Topography, then, combines a knowledge of the terrain, its monuments, and archeological evidence with that of the historical written sources. Correctly interpreted, they illuminate one another and thus make essential contributions to such fields as archeology, whether classical, post-classical, or medieval; to the history of city planning; and to religious, military, social, and also general history.

The identification of a building through historical sources is not too inspiring, except for the specialist. It becomes more stimulating within a broader context as one probes deeper into the evidence, both archeological and historical, to explore the reasons—more than one as a rule—for a given site's being occupied by a particular building. These reasons are usually very down to earth: easy access by land or water; a preexistent street system; the commercial value of the site, which may be on a street corner or near a marketplace or on a much-traveled thoroughfare; or the defensive strength of the location. Or else the lot has been for a long time in the hands of the owner, be it an individual or a corporation:

large numbers of churches in Rome rise over or incorporate the remains of private houses or tenements that, from literary evidence, appear to have served as meeting houses for Christian congregations long before these churches were built. Beyond these practical reasons for the location of a building, other factors must be taken into consideration. A building may have been erected on a particular site so as to eradicate the memory of a structure formerly in that place: a contemporary source reports at length how Bishop Porphyry in 401 had the great sanctuary of Gaza demolished stone by stone and replaced by a church in cross shape on the same site. Alternatively, a church may commemorate a site or an object long held sacred by the Christian community and thus ensure its continued veneration: the basilica on the Vatican Hill over the grave of Saint Peter; the church in St. Catherine's monastery on Mount Sinai on the site of the Burning Bush; the Anastasis Rotunda in Jerusalem enclosing the Holy Sepulchre, since the time of Constantine held to be Christ's tomb. The evidence for identifying the object of veneration and hence the site obviously varies in historical value from case to case. At times, as in the instance of St. Peter's, both written sources and archeological remains clearly identify the site; at other times—one thinks of Mount Sinai—the evidence can only be legendary and based on vague oral tradition.

The cathedral of Rome, S. Giovanni in Laterano, founded by Constantine in 312, does not shelter any saint's grave, nor did it prior to the High Middle Ages house any other object of veneration that could have determined the peculiar location of the church near the walls of the city, in what in the fourth century was a quiet zone of large mansions and parks. Practical considerations were, to be sure, not entirely disregarded: a suitable building ground, sufficiently large, was provided by demolishing a sizable military camp. But the area was far removed from the populous quarters of the city and hence most inconvenient of access for the large Christian congregation of Rome. To explain the choice of site, the historian's net must be cast wide. Contemporary writings, both Christian and pagan, Constantine's own legislation, inscriptions, and coins provide the clues. Interpreted and weighed against one another, they suggest that Constantine's aim in placing the Lateran church far out was to avoid or minimize friction with a strong pagan opposition headed by the Senate and the old families—an opposition that necessitated keeping at a safe distance from the city's center, crowded with pagan sanctuaries under their protection. For the same reason the church was laid out on property at the emperor's free disposal: Christianity, as viewed at this time by Constantine, was to a large degree his personal affair; and correspondingly the Church stood under his powerful, but personal, protection. Likewise, St. Peter's and other Constantinian church foundations rose, outside the city walls beyond the Senate's jurisdiction, and on Constantine's and his family's private property. A very real political motive, together with equally real political ideologies, underlies the topographical choices for his church buildings erected in the first decade of his rule under the particular circumstances obtaining in Rome.

The interplay of historical evidence—written sources, legislation, inscriptions, and numismatics—and of available archeological testimony likewise leads toward a meaningful interpretation of the siting of outstanding churches and monuments in Constantinople, Constantine's new capital. The cathedral, H. Sophia, now replaced by Justinian's church, was made to occupy the most prominent point of the city, together with the palace, the circus, and other government structures. The choice of the site by itself thus suggests what historical evidence confirms: the political situation of both the emperor and the Church had radically changed since the foundation fourteen years earlier of the Lateran cathedral on private imperial property at the outer edge of Rome. At Constantinople, Constantine was in full control of the city, as he was, by then, of the empire. No pagan opposition existed in his new capital; and elsewhere it had been silenced. Constantine had taken the Church under his official protection and had incorporated it into the state, so much so as to subject it to his will. Beyond that, Constantine's view of himself and of the emperor's overpowering place in the scheme of a Christian universe was mirrored in the location within the city of two further monuments planned by him and closely linked to the image held of himself: the column, set up at the hinge of the old and the new city, carrying his statue in the guise of the New Helios, Christ; and the layout, in the image of Christ's Sepulchre in Jerusalem, of his own grave in the church of the Holy Apostles, the only church building completed in Constantinople during his lifetime. Both in Rome in 312 and in Constantinople in 326, then, the choice of building sites and with it the topography of the city were interwoven with and influenced by considerations of a political nature, whether founded on reality or on ideological motives.

The elements of such a "political topography," to coin a term, underlie as well situations differing from Constantine's with regard to both time and political ideologies. One thinks of the Roman citizenry's relocation of the seat of the city government on the Capitoline Hill in the twelfth century, a choice confirmed three and four centuries later and visually stressed by Michelangelo's palaces enveloping the *area Capitolina*; or one recalls L'Enfant's siting of the Capitol in Washington, D.C., at the very center of his city plan. For this book I have chosen, in addition to Constantine's foundations at Rome and Constantinople, two more case histories from Late Antiquity: Milan around 380, at the time of St. Ambrose; and Rome under papal rule from the late fourth to the mid-fifth century. In all four the siting of buildings and monuments is determined by what today is called power politics, with the understanding, however, that the forces involved are either temporal or spiritual but in either case political in their effects. At Rome in 312, at the beginning of his rule over the Western Empire, Constantine had to navigate between forces of very different natures and strengths: on the one hand, the very real presence of a locally powerful pagan Senate and the resulting need of conciliatory action; on the other hand, his equally real need to come to terms with the God of Christianity, his new faith but dimly perceived, and to take His Church under the Imperial wing. Fourteen years later at Constantinople the confrontation took place on a plane that was purely ideological but equally loaded with political connotations: Constantine, possessed of fundamentally incompatible convictions, his profound Christian faith and his belief in his Imperial station, confronted the issue, insoluble for him, of reconciling the lingering persuasion of his own divinity qua emperor with the concept of Christ as the One God and Emperor of the Universe. Much in contrast, the situation in Milan around 380 was dominated by political realities, though linked to both religious and political concepts. The cathedral in the heart of the city was held by Ambrose, the Catholic bishop; a strong "heretical" faction at court, at least tolerated by the emperor Gratian, built the church of S. Lorenzo as a "counter cathedral," near the palace but beyond the city walls, presumably to minimize friction. The situation compares with that obtaining in Rome when the Lateran cathedral was founded, with the obvious difference that at Milan the opposing parties were both Christian. Interwoven with the religious issues and underlying Ambrose's battle for the possession of the new church was his stand against the temporal power's interfering in matters ecclesiastical. By the turn of the fifth century the fight was won. The emperor, at least in the West, no longer had a voice in the Church. Conversely, the Church herself had become a temporal power ruling Rome and weighty in matters secular in large parts of the West. The changing topography of the city of Rome reflected both this situation and an emerging new conflict. New church buildings rising all over town mirrored the image of a Rome by then emphatically Christian and ruled by the Church. Yet the location of the cathedral and the bishop's residence established by Constantine at the Lateran isolated the bishop from the population, the more so since the city, shrinking as it was, was moving away from the Lateran, while focusing on Saint Peter's tomb and his basilica: hence the bishop's endeavors to reach out toward his flock by sumptuous church buildings and by liturgical changes; hence also the attempt to stake out by "subsidiary cathedrals" around the Lateran, splendidly refurbished, a papal quarter in the image of imperial residences. Topography and political aims interlocked and their interweaving was mirrored by the visual evidence.

The essays in this small volume attempt to explore the possibilities of such a political topography. Monuments and sites on the one hand and written evidence on the other are employed so as to illuminate one another with the aim of sketching the political atmosphere of the historical circumstances. Whether the visual evidence or the written testimony prevails in elucidating this relationship changes from case to case. Also it is hard in retrospect to establish whether, in building the argument, the starting point has been the site chosen or the political background against which the choice should be seen. In any event, the preliminary character of the following four essays should be kept in mind throughout.

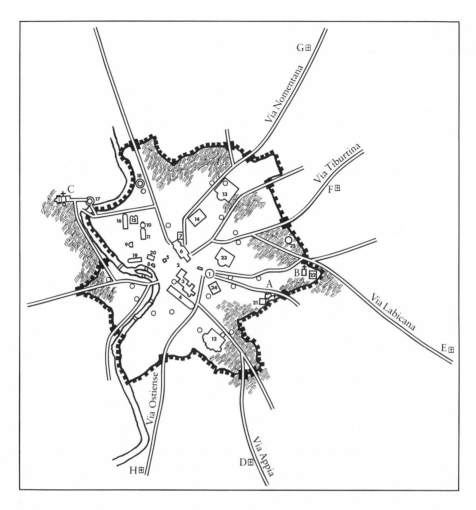

ANCIENT MONUMENTS
1 Colosseum
2 Forum
3 Palatine
4 Circus Maximus
5 Capitol
6 Imperial Fora
7 Market of Trajan
8 Theatre of Marcellus
9 Theatre of Pompey
10 Pantheon
11 Thermae of Agrippa
12 Thermae of Caracalla
13 Thermae of Diocletian
14 Thermae of Constantine

15 Thermae of Alex. Severus
16 Stadium of Domitian
   (Piazza Navona)
17 Mausoleum of Hadrian
   (Castel S. Angelo)
18 Mausoleum of Augustus
19 Circus Flaminius
20 Porticus of Octavia
21 Castra Equitum
   Singularium
22 Sessorium
23 Thermae of Trajan
24 Claudianum
25 Minerva Medica

CHRISTIAN BUILDINGS

o Tituli

🛉 Churches:
   A Lateran basilica
   B S. Croce

⊞ Covered cemeteries and
martyr's churches:
   C St. Peter's
   D S. Sebastiano
   E SS. Marcellino e Pietro
   F S. Lorenzo
   G S. Agnese
   H Shrine of Saint Paul

 GARDENS

1. The Rome of Constantine, 330 A.D.

I

ROME

The map of Rome on October 28, 312, the day Constantine defeated
Maxentius at *saxa rubra*—or, as the battle is commonly called, the Milvian Bridge—and entered Rome as uncontested sole ruler of the western
half of the Empire, is fairly well known (fig. 1).[1] The towered walls built
forty years before by the emperors Aurelian and Probus, hence named
the Aurelian Walls, are well preserved to this day for their total length of
twelve miles, roughly eighteen kilometers, ringing on the east bank of the
Tiber the greater part of the old city, and on the west bank *trans Tibe-
rim*, Trastevere (fig. 2). Roads from all over the known world entered
through sixteen gates, major and minor, and continued as main arteries
to the center of the city, its monumental and administrative show area,
ideally still the heart of the Empire. There, Romans and foreigners alike
gawked at the symbols of Rome's power: on the Capitol the temples of
Jupiter and Juno; on the Palatine the imperial palaces, still the official
residences of the emperors when in Rome. Below the Capitol and Palatine sprawled the Roman Forum with its temples, statues, and triumphal
arches (fig. 3), with the Curia of the Senate and the Basilica Julia, both
rebuilt by Diocletian around 285, and with the newest and grandest
additions, laid out between 306 and 312 by Maxentius, barely completed: the Temple of Venus and Roma, entirely rebuilt by him; a hall,
now housing the church of SS. Cosma e Damiano but originally, it is
presumed, the audience hall of the city prefect, preceded by a domed
round vestibule (fig. 4); and, located between the two, the Basilica Nova,
its massive walls and coffered vaulting still towering high over the east-

ward rise of the Via Sacra (fig. 5). Further east beyond that rise, the Colosseum, built late in the first century, to this day stands to its full height
(fig. 6). North of the Forum Romanum extended side by side the Imperial Fora laid out from Caesar and Augustus to Vespasian, Nerva,
and Trajan—the latter the grandest and dominated by his basilica, temple, and column; its forecourt expanded in huge hemicycles, the one
to the right surmounted by the Market of Trajan, a high-rise structure
where rows of shops on every floor opened on vaulted and unvaulted
passages (fig. 7). Beyond the Capitol spread the Campus Martius, northward to the Mausoleum of Augustus, westward to the Tiber bridge crossing the river to the Mausoleum of Hadrian, Castel S. Angelo (fig. 8), and
southward to the foot of the Aventine. It was a show area covered with
temples, theatres, circuses, and thermae: the Circus Maximus and the
Pantheon, the Theatre of Pompey and the Stadium of Domitian—now
Piazza Navona—, the Thermae of Alexander Severus between the Pantheon and Piazza Navona, the Theatre of Marcellus, and nearby the Porticus of Octavia and the Circus Flaminius. That area, covering roughly
one-fourth of the entire surface of the city, was all marble and gilding
and, one fears, as pretentious as today's Monumento Vittoriano on
Piazza Venezia.

Removed from this spectacular display of grandeur, those who held
power lived in a greenbelt that ran along the Aurelian Walls, both inside
and out. Their mansions, loosely adjoining one another in gardens and
parks, spread in a wide crescent across the hills, where the air was good
and cool, from the Pincio to the Quirinal and Esquiline, to the Celian
and the Aventine, and across the river to the Gianicolo. The huge garden
pavilion, misnamed the Minerva Medica, no longer embedded in green-
ery as it still was a century ago, but in a depressing neighborhood by the
railway yards (fig. 9); the ruins of the Gardens of Sallustius, similarly
deteriorating, not far from Via Vittorio Veneto; the remains of the Sessorian Palace by S. Croce in Gerusalemme, near the walls at the southeastern edge of the city; and those of another luxury villa buried below
the Bibliotheca Hertziana in the northern sector of town—these still
mark the sites of such palatial mansions, many imperial property by the
early fourth century.[2] All told, the greenbelt of ancient Rome seventeen
hundred years ago was not unlike that which still enveloped the town in
the nineteenth century, before the huge villas and parks of the great
Roman families—the Aldobrandini, the Ludovisi, and the Massimi—or
the olive groves and vineyards of wealthy convents, such as those of
SS. Giovanni e Paolo south of the Colosseum, fell prey to building speculation (fig.10). Around A.D. 300 that garden zone, with its aristocratic
and imperial mansions and with plenty of building sites available, also
sheltered the two largest thermae of third-century date, those of Cara-

4. Rome, Forum Romanum, audience hall of city prefect, now SS. Cosma e Damiano, vestibule rotunda, ca. 320

2. Rome, Aurelian Walls

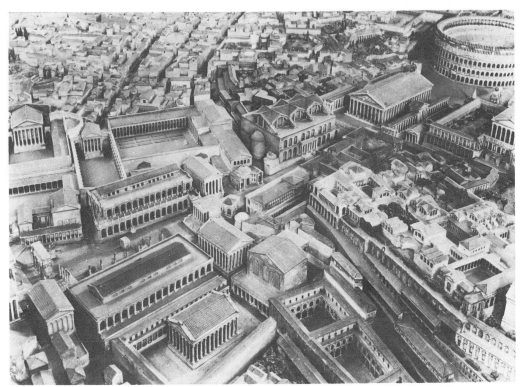

3. Rome, Forum Romanum, Palatine, and Imperial Fora as of ca. 320, *From left: foreground*, Basilica Julia, "southwest" building, Palatine with imperial palaces; *middle ground*, Basilica Aemilia, Temple of Antoninus and Faustina, hall of the city prefect, Basilica Nova (of Maxentius or Constantine), Temple of Venus and Roma, Colosseum; *background*, Forum of Augustus, Forum of Nerva (Forum Transitorium), Forum of Vespasian (Templum Pacis).

5. Rome, Basilica Nova (of Maxentius or Constantine), north side

6. Rome, Temple of Venus and Roma (foreground) and Colosseum

7. Rome, Forum of Trajan, hemicycle, and, *above*, Market of Trajan

8. Rome, Castel Sant'Angelo (Mausoleum of Hadrian) and bridge

calla and Diocletian, and for reasons of both space and security the huge barracks of the troops stationed in or passing through Rome.

Squeezed between the greenbelt and the great show area, clustered in the valleys between the hills and in the low parts of town, the *città bassa* along the river, in Trastevere, and around Monte Testaccio, always threatened by floods and epidemics, the mass of the population lived in hovels, houses, and tenements of all sizes, shapes, and building materials—many solidly constructed, four and more stories high and eight or nine bays long; others small and jerry-built (fig. 11). Such tenements (*insulae*)—as a rule housing shops, bakeries, workshops, or small bathing establishments on the ground floor—lined narrow alleys, smelly and noisy as to this day at Naples or Fez, dark, crowded, often spanned by arches, as they still are seen on the Clivus Scauri and here and there in Trastevere (fig. 12). Occasionally a mansion, small or large, had inserted itself or remained from earlier times engulfed by the ever-spreading zones of tenements. Such tenements, indeed, extended long offshoots into both the greenbelt and the show area: the walls of three large tenements survive incorporated in the fabric of SS. Giovanni e Paolo on the Clivus Scauri among the villas on the Celian Hill; the ruin of another stands at the very foot of the Capitol; still others are built into the church of S. Anastasia below the Palatine—both in the heart of the monumental center of Rome. As to this day in the old city, the Costaguti and the little cobbler, the rich and the poor, public building and squalor lived side by side.

The great marble plan of Rome of early third-century date and the *regionaria*, fourth-century gazetteers, jointly convey a fair idea of the narrow streets, the *insulae* with ground-floor shops, and the intermingling of luxury and beggary.[3] The very number of tenements and hovels and of mansions and parks, the gilded splendor of temples and public buildings, the Fora and the streets, and the labyrinth of the hundreds of narrow alleys reflected a Rome which still remained in the mind of contemporaries, traditionalists and innovators alike, the true *caput mundi*. She still was the only legitimate capital of the Empire, notwithstanding the new imperial residences all over—York and Trier, Milan and Nicomedia, Thessalonikē and Antioch—whence ever since the latter part of the third century successive emperors had actually governed the Empire.

This was what Rome looked like when Constantine conquered the city. Shortly after, he decided to build a cathedral for the Christian community of Rome and its bishop, presumably as an ex-voto to Christ, who had granted him victory: the εὐχαριστήριον which Constantine, so Eusebius tells, "forthwith offered as an εὐχὴ," a vow, was perhaps this cathedral rather than a mere thanksgiving prayer. The *dedicatio*, the act of foundation, of renouncing the property, would have fallen certainly

9. Rome, Minerva Medica as of 1820, drawing F. J. B. Kobell

11. Rome, tenement house, foot of Capitoline Hill, model

10. Rome, Colosseum as of ca. 1870 from the south, showing olive groves and gardens

12. Rome, Clivus Scauri spanned by arches and SS. Giovanni e Paolo

14. Rome, S. Giovanni in Laterano, foundation wall of Constantinian nave

13. Rome, S. Giovanni in Laterano as of ca. 1860

into the winter of 312; perhaps, in fact—but this is conjectural—it took place as early as November 9, thirteen days after the conquest, forthwith indeed.[4] As the site for the building, the emperor chose an area on the Celian Hill far out in the southeastern corner of the city and just inside the walls. Thus it was to rise among the affluent mansions of the green-belt, in a garden zone, more or less as it still rose a hundred years ago (fig. 13).[5] By 312 some of the mansions nearby had long been the emperor's private property, such as that confiscated by Nero from the Laterani family—hence the name of the area—or the two adjoining villas of Marcus Aurelius's mother and his grandfather, where his equestrian statue stood until transferred first a few hundred yards away to the front of the papal palace, then in 1538 by Michelangelo to the Capitol. Amidst these mansions, a huge square was occupied by the *castra equitum singularium*, the barracks of the imperial horse guards. The corps may have fought on the wrong side, that of Maxentius; in any event it was cashiered by 313. The barracks were confiscated and razed, the cleared site was filled in, and the Lateran Cathedral, now S. Giovanni in Laterano, was built. Work was begun, I submit, as early as the spring of 313; construction proceeded rapidly, and the *consecratio*, the transfer of the ex-voto gift from the realm of the *profanum* to the deity, Christ in that case, may have taken place on November 9, 318, six years after its foundation: a reasonably long period of construction, given the seven to nine years it took to complete construction work and start on the decoration of the much larger church of St. Peter. Getting the Lateran cathedral ready for consecration may well have taken four more years.[6]

What today stand out in S. Giovanni in Laterano are, to be sure, the monumental eighteenth-century façade and the interior, designed and remodeled by Borromini between 1646 and 1650, one of his grandest and most sophisticated creations. However, Constantine's church was by no means all destroyed. Large parts survive below the present floor level or incorporated into Borromini's fabric, and they have been brought to light in successive campaigns of research over the past fifty years. The foundation walls of apse, nave, and aisles have been uncovered, sunk down between the walls of the barracks, which they cut and traverse to a depth of over 7.50 meters; they are solidly built of large chunks of stone, heavily cemented and 1.70 meters thick (fig. 14). Fragments of the nave pavement, composed of large, colored marble plaques, were found in the thirties and are known from photographs. Above ground, stretches of wall still rise 8.50 meters high, built of brickfaced mortared rubble (*opus caementicium*) and showing remains of aisle windows and doors. Moreover, numerous scattered fragments, both structural and decorative, have been unearthed, among the former a spandrel from the aisle arcades. Survey drawings of the church as it stood until 1646, done by Borromini himself in his precise, elegant hand and by assistants, as well as early descriptions, further clarify plan, interior, and decoration of Constantine's basilica. The nave, 100 meters (333⅓ Roman feet) long, terminated in an apse and was flanked on either side by twin aisles, separated by arcades, the width totaling over 53 meters, roughly 180 Roman feet (fig. 15). Wings, possibly depositories for offerings, projected in the chancel area from the inner aisles. A raised pathway enclosed by parapets, a *solea*, for the bishop's solemn entry into his church, led to the chancel. Nineteen tall, slender, trabeated columns on either side carried the nave walls; a set of forty-two green marble columns divided the aisles. The inner aisles were probably higher than the outer ones, and both, aisles and nave, were lit by large windows—a fresco painted in 1650, though a reconstruction and unreliable on some points, nonetheless conveys an impression of the slender colonnades and the abundant lighting (fig. 16).[7] The decoration was splendidly colorful: the nave columns red granite; green columns in the aisles; marble revetment on the aisle arcade and perhaps on the walls; the nave marble-paved; an aniconic mosaic, apparently sheer gold foil, in the apse; a silver *fastigium*; a screen or canopy, on the chord of the apse, carrying silver-sheathed statues of Christ, angels, and apostles, a remarkably early example of figural church decoration; and chandeliers and candlesticks of silver and gold all over. Behind the church an octagonal baptistery was built, and nearby a residence was found for the bishop and his staff, whether the mansion uncovered some two hundred meters behind the apse, or one closer to the façade, whence he could conveniently make his solemn entrance into the cathedral.[8]

Clearly, the basilica at the Lateran broke with the tradition of the buildings that so far had and for quite a while continued to serve Christian worship all over the Empire: *domus ecclesiae*, community centers, or *tituli*, as named in Rome. The best and, in fact, the only thoroughly known to this day is the one found in the 1920s at Dura-Europos on the Euphrates frontier: a small residence, adapted as early as A.D. 230 for the religious and administrative needs of a small congregation (fig. 17).[9] Like the one at Dura, other *domus ecclesiae* were houses of local type, purchased by the congregations or donated by a wealthy member. Adapted to their new function as best possible, they sheltered under one roof a meeting room for services, classrooms to instruct postulants and catechumens, a baptistery, offices, quarters for the clergy, closets to store food and clothing for the poor, and, in a wealthy congregation's *domus*, a reception room for the bishop. Only rarely and at a late date may a congregation have been in a position to own a hall set aside for services only, such as, in Rome, the one buried next to S. Crisogono in Trastevere, built presumably around 310 under the tolerant re-

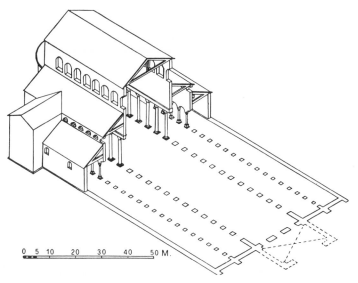

15. Rome, S. Giovanni in Laterano, Constantinian basilica, reconstruction

16. Rome, S. Giovanni in Laterano, interior, reconstruction, fresco G. B. Gagliardi, 1650, S. Martino al Monti

gime of Maxentius. But as a rule Christian congregations through the
fourth century continued to use, to acquire, and to adapt to their needs
ordinary houses as they became available: a small town residence, as at
Dura; a hall in the garden of an elegant mansion, such as the one found
below S. Pietro in Vincoli (fig. 18); a large room in a villa, as at S. Sabina
in Rome; or an apartment in a tenement like the one incorporated into
the foundations and side wall of SS. Giovanni e Paolo. In any event, they
were emphatically private, modest in size, and utilitarian in function.[10]

The Lateran cathedral was of a different kind. Designed for worship
only, it was huge, holding three thousand or more faithful; quarters for
the clergy, offices, and even the baptistery became separate structures.
Thus isolated, the church was monumental, rising high over its surroundings, just as it still did a hundred years ago; and it claimed by its size, its
splendor, and its very building type public rather than private standing.[11]
Indeed, while breaking with past Christian building tradition, Constantine's cathedral was deeply rooted in the mainstream of Roman public
architecture. Its plan, design, and overall function were evolved within
the genus of the public assembly hall, the basilica, as, over many centuries, it had sprouted up all over the Roman commonwealth with ever-
new variations in form and function: riding academies and bazaars;
theatre lobbies and halls to see clients, discuss business, or dispense law;
meeting rooms for religious sects; reception halls in the mansions of the
great; courts of magistrates; and imperial audience halls where the living
god revealed himself to his subjects. Such basilicas could be spartan as a
drill hall in a military camp or grand as Trajan's Basilica Ulpia (fig. 19);
single-naved or with aisles, or with three, two, or one or without apses;
with bare walls or with marble columns and gilding and shimmering in
multicolored *opus sectile*—all depending on local tradition, specific
function, and available means. Religious overtones, ever inherent in
public building through the obligatory presence of a divinity's or the
emperor's effigy, by the fourth century had turned into a sanctuary of
the Divine Majesty the emperor's audience hall, where his faithful con-
gregated to adore him. Hence, the type of these audience halls quickly
gained ascendance within the overall genus basilica: single-naved, apsed,
profusely lit, glittering with marble, painting, mosaic and gilding—as
witness the seat of the city prefect on the Forum Romanum (fig. 20) and
on a still grander scale Constantine's audience hall in Trier, built but a
few years before the Lateran cathedral (fig. 21).

The Lateran cathedral, then, was, generally speaking, but another variant on the genus assembly hall, basilica. Within that genus it was adapted
to its proper task, to its particular standing as Constantine's donation
and to its function as the throne room of the Heavenly King. Hence it
was designed to conform to the requirements of Christian ritual as prac-

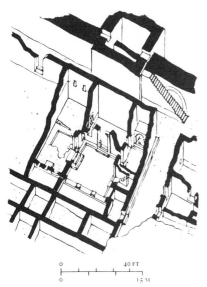

17. Dura-Europos, Christian meeting house (*domus ecclesiae*), reconstruction

18. Rome, garden hall below S. Pietro in Vincoli, reconstruction

19. Rome, Basilica Ulpia, interior, reconstruction

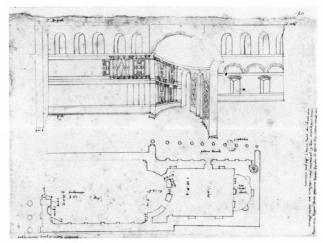

20. Rome, audience hall of city prefect(?), now SS. Cosma
e Damiano, interior and plan as of ca. 1550, drawing
P. Ligorio

ticed in Rome, to the needs of both speedy construction and lavish
splendor as urged by the donor, and to the concept of its being the seat
of Christ, Emperor in Heaven. Laid out lengthwise, it was focused on the
apse where the bishop was enthroned, Christ's magistrate as it were, and
on the altar where in the sacrifice of the Mass Christ revealed Himself to
His people. Since no single-naved hall could have held a congregation as
large as that to be gathered in the Roman cathedral, the plan was expanded sideways by twin aisles. Lastly, its size and splendor, the osten-
tation of gilding, mosaic, marble, gold, and silver, would proclaim the
generosity and riches of the exalted imperial donor, the status of the
Church he patronized, and the greatness of Christ, who resided within
as *basileus* Supreme. Ever since the first and second centuries, indeed,
Christ had been viewed as Ruler All-High, King and Emperor. Around
314 Eusebius, in formulas borrowed from Roman Imperial terminology,
styled Him "Sovereign *basileus* of the Universe, Law Giver Supreme,
ever victorious"; His silver-sheathed statue in Majesty, enthroned and
guarded by spear-carrying angels, faced the bishop seated in the apse of
the Lateran, while the congregation saw Him as teacher, flanked by the
apostles; and, nearly a century later, the mosaic at S. Pudenziana shows
Him as *basileus* enthroned, His hand raised in the *adlocutio* gesture,
wearing the purple gold-woven dress of the emperor, and flanked by the
apostles in senatorial garb (fig. 22).[12] To fourth-century men, then, the
Lateran cathedral and Constantine's other churches would evoke most
closely within the genus basilica the emperor's audience halls and,
beyond that, imperial palaces in general.[13]

21. Trier, basilica (*sedes iustitiae*), interior

22. Rome, S. Pudenziana, mosaic, Christ
enthroned

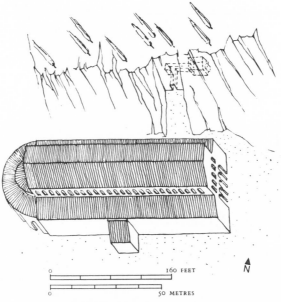

23. Rome, S. Lorenzo fuori le Mura, covered cemetery
and catacomb chamber, reconstruction

By implication, then, Constantine's churches claimed official standing. In 325–26 he himself, in a letter to bishop Makarios of Jerusalem, stressed the claim: the church at the Holy Sepulchre was to be "a basilica not only more beautiful than others anywhere, but such that in all respects the beauties of any city shall yield to this building." [14] In fact, all the churches he and the ladies of the imperial house built in Rome over the fifteen-odd years following his conquest of the city implicitly aspired to public standing. All were large. All were richly provided with precious fittings. All were lavishly endowed, their income for maintenance alone totaling nearly 25,000 gold solidi. [15] All were variants on that eminently public type, the basilica, like the Lateran cathedral. But all differed both in function and in plan from that, Constantine's first church foundation in Rome, as well as from each other. Rising near the catacombs sheltering the graves of Saint Lawrence, Saint Agnes, Saints Marcellinus and Peter the Deacon, and over a shrine commemorating the Apostles Peter and Paul *ad catacumbas* (now S. Sebastiano), they served as covered cemeteries and funerary banquet halls: longitudinal in plan, the floor carpeted with graves, the aisles enveloping the apse ambulatory-fashion, often with mausolea crowding around; S. Lorenzo fuori le Mura may serve as an example (fig. 23). Sometimes they would be linked to an imperial mausoleum: at S. Agnese, that of Constantine's daughter Constantina, now S. Constanza; at SS. Marcellino e Pietro that of Helena, probably Constantine's own to start with and ceded to his mother once he moved to Constantinople. St. Peter's, combining as it did the function of a martyr's shrine with that of a funerary hall, was provided with twin aisles flanking the nave and with a low transept and apse to shelter the apostle's grave; the remains of the nave until the early seventeenth century conveyed an idea of the size and monumentality of Constantinian church building (fig. 24). At S. Croce in Gerusalemme a single nave was spanned by two sets of triple arches, the latter inserted when, probably in the early 320s, a third-century hall in the Sessorian Palace was converted into the palace church of the empress dowager and her court; a relic of the True Cross, perhaps brought by her from her visit to the Holy Land in 326–27, was sheltered either in the church proper or in an adjoining room under a canopy which, as has been recently suggested, copied that placed by Constantine over the Sepulchre of Christ in Jerusalem (fig. 25). [16] All these churches, then, rose on estates which were part of the patrimony that over the centuries had accumulated in the hands of the emperors' privy purse, the *res privata*: S. Lorenzo on the *Ager Veranus* along the Via Tiburtina, ever since Lucius Verus (died 168) imperial property; S. Agnese on the grounds of the villa of Constantine's daughter Constantina-Constantia on the Via Nomentana; SS. Marcellino e Pietro on Helena's estate *ad duas lauros* on the Via Labicana; the build-

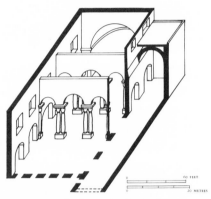

24. Rome, Old St. Peter's (and crossing of New St. Peter's) as of 1536, drawing M. van Heemskerck

25. Rome, S. Croce in Gerusalemme, reconstruction

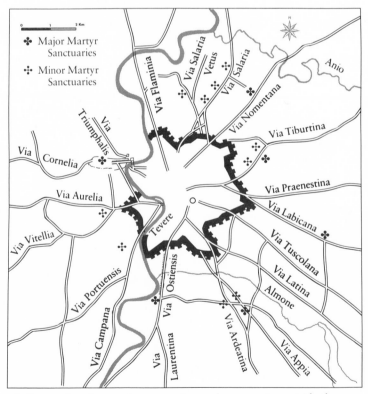

26. Rome, showing roads, cemeteries, and sanctuaries outside the walls

ing *ad catacumbas*, S. Sebastiano, along the Appia on an estate left, one supposes, by Herodes Atticus to the privy purse; St. Peter's in the Gardens of Nero across the Tiber, not far from a branch of the Via Cassia; lastly S. Croce inside the Sessorian Palace. All, then, rose on private estates withdrawn, as it were, from the general public (fig. 26). Yet all, through their size, their riches, their splendor, indeed through the very fact of belonging to that eminently public architectural order, the basilica, claimed to rival public building. There is, it seems, an inherent contradiction at the very basis of Constantine's church foundations in Rome.

One thinks all too readily of Constantine as the Christian emperor and of the churches he built or is supposed to have built in Rome and elsewhere. But Constantine first and foremost was a Roman emperor, and a Roman emperor was obliged to show his grandeur and power by setting up huge and showy public buildings—public not by implication, but in a very real sense. Constantine did not evade this responsibility.[17] In Rome, on the Quirinal he erected as early as around 315 a huge thermae building. Its ruins, still upright in part in the late sixteenth century (fig. 27), have been traced over a length of more than two hundred meters and a width of at least one hundred meters, extending from the site of Palazzo Rospigliosi and the Consultà on the crest of the Quirinal southwards to that of the Banca d'Italia off Piazza Magnanapoli—the southern end supported on a huge terrace and the whole structure burying under its vast expanse large numbers of earlier buildings abandoned for its sake: warehouses, perhaps tenements, and certainly half a dozen or more private residences lavishly appointed. Inside its domed and vaulted halls the thermae sheltered a wealth of statuary, some from

27. Rome, Thermae of Constantine on Quirinal as of 1575, engraving E. Du Pérac

the outset, others accumulated in the later fourth century—the horse tamers, statues of Constantine and his sons, the river-gods now on the Capitol, conquered barbarians (fig. 28). Nearby, perhaps in the *porticus Constantini*, a colonnaded hall adjoining the thermae, the bronze statues of a Hellenistic ruler and of a seated boxer were found some eighty years ago. On the Roman Forum in Carolingian times still rose an equestrian statue of Constantine. The Basilica of Maxentius was altered and redecorated by Constantine: in the apse at the west end of the nave his colossal statue was set up right after his conquest of Rome; its fragments, found in situ, and the head in particular now dominate the courtyard of the Palazzo dei Conservatori (see below, fig. 32). Subsequently a new apse was built onto the north flank of the nave to shelter the tribunal, formerly in the west apse, and a new entrance porch was added facing south towards the palaces on the Palatine. Near the basilica, the presumed audience hall of the city prefect and its domed vestibule too may have been completed by Constantine. Likewise, on the Forum Boarium a huge tetrapylon, misnamed the Janus Quadrifrons, seems to have been built by Constantine (fig. 29). The Circus Maximus at the foot of the Palatine he restored "with gilded columns and high porticoes." The obelisk now at the Lateran he had brought from Thebes to Alexandria to be set up on the *spina* of the circus, but its transfer to Rome and its erection took place only in 357 under his son Constantius II. Finally, there is of course the triumphal arch by the Colosseum, built largely from pilfered material and dedicated to Constantine in 315 by the Senate to glorify the victory at *saxa rubra* (fig. 30).[18]

All these monuments built or completed by or dedicated to Constantine were in a real sense public buildings, *opera publica* in legal language, like the temples, theatres, administrative structures, and thermae built by earlier emperors and officials. Their legal standing coincided with the claims raised by their size, their architectural genus, and the splendor of their furnishings. They were Constantine's contribution as Roman emperor to the display of imperial bounty in brick and marble in the heart of the one legitimate capital of the Empire. Likewise, his official seal was imprinted by him or by a willing Senate on the great public buildings left by the defeated Maxentius: his basilica, the Basilica Nova, naturally took Constantine's name, as it sheltered his statue; inscriptions proclaimed Constantine the builder of the audience hall of the city prefect, if that is what SS. Cosma e Damiano was; and a senate decree attributed to him the rebuilding of the Temple of Venus and Roma, just completed by Maxentius. As behooved a Roman emperor, Constantine by the Senate's decision took over the monumental center of Rome and of her Empire.

The more noticeable, then, is the siting of his foundations for the Christian community of the city. After all, they too were grand show

28. Rome, Quirinal, horse tamers and
other statuary, as of 1546, painting
M. van Heemskerck, detail

29. Rome, Janus Quadritrons

30. Rome, Arch of Constantine from the north

pieces—huge, glittering with marble and mosaic, rising high, splendidly furnished and richly endowed. Clearly they were designed to rival public architecture and imperial palaces. Still, none rise in or remotely near the center of the city, where they would visually compete with such structures and be seen by everybody. The martyrs' churches, to be sure, were *eo ipso* located outside the Aurelian Walls, *fuori le mura*. The graves and cemeteries on which they rose, like all burial places, were banished by Roman law from within the city limits—the Servian Wall prior to the building of the Aurelian Walls, the latter afterwards by custom, if not by law. The placing of S. Croce in Gerusalemme inside the Sessorian Palace likewise makes sense; it was after all the palatine church of the empress dowager. But to find the cathedral of Rome on the very edge of the city, hidden away in the greenbelt, demands an explanation. The location could hardly have been more inconvenient. On the great feast days—at Easter in particular, but also at Christmas—the faithful by the thousands would have to trudge out there, an hour's walk or sometimes more. Only the bishop, after all, could impart baptism, and only at Easter. The site was equally inconvenient for the episcopal administration. Communication with the parishes all over the city, from the northern Campus Martius to Trastevere, was difficult and time-consuming. The clergy may well have complained among themselves about the whim of His Majesty in choosing that faraway site, the Lateran. But then, the new cathedral was a gift horse. Anyhow, did one remonstrate with the emperor's Divine Majesty?

Constantine, though, had good reasons for selecting a remote location for this his first church foundation. They were alluded to forty years ago by Schönebeck and elaborated on by Alföldi in his still superb *Conversion of Constantine*.[19] Politically and religiously the center of Rome was sensitive ground. On the Capitol, on the Forum and in the Imperial Fora, and on the Campus Martius and southward stood the temples of the gods who for a thousand years had protected Rome. There, too, stood the basilicas, theatres, thermae, and imperial mausolea, nearly all provided with shrines for major and minor divinities and for emperors raised among the gods. There sat the Senate in the Curia, sheltering the altar of Victory, still fervently defended half a century later; there in their administrative buildings sat the magistrates appointed from among the great Roman families. All these structures had been founded by members of the same families or by emperors, and they were maintained by their descendants and successors in office. To place next to such structures the basilica designed for the Christian congregation was out of the question, even if suitable ground could have been found. It would have been a major challenge to the Senate and the traditionalists among the Romans, from among both the upper and the lower classes. Keeping his first church foundation and indeed all later ones as far as possible from the center of Rome, because of the predominance of conservative and religiously traditional groups both in the Senate and among the population, was by necessity, in 312–13 certainly, but for some years to come as well, an integral part of Constantine's building policy. The sanctuaries outside the walls at the graves of the martyrs and of Saint Peter could not hurt anybody's feelings. Nor could S. Croce, hidden inside the Sessorian Palace, possibly offend the susceptibilities of even the most fervent upholder of the old faith. Only the cathedral at the Lateran rose in the open, as it were, inside the city walls. Still, like S. Croce, it remained outside the *pomoerium*, the religious boundary marked by the old Republican, the so-called Servian, Wall and still respected after the building much further out of the Aurelian Walls. Where the Lateran cathedral rose, half an hour's walk or more from the sensitive area in the city's center with its pagan overtones, it would at least not blatantly insult conservative pagan feeling.

It was as part of a policy of sparing pagan sentiment that Constantine, as he did in Rome, placed his and his family's church foundations on their own estates, beyond the walls and inside the Sessorian Palace. On his own ground everyone was free to do as he pleased. Moreover, while accessible to any faithful from among the Christian community in Rome willing to walk a few miles or to an occasional pilgrim come from afar, these funerary halls, like the graves of the martyrs nearby, would draw worshippers primarily from among the vast households settled on the estates and from country folk living close by. Certainly at S. Croce in Gerusalemme, the congregation by and large was confined to those living in the palace and on its grounds. Non-Christians were obviously aware of the buildings Constantine was setting up on his own estates: funerary halls, martyrs' shrines, a palace church. But they could and would ignore their existence. Surely, they were no concern of the authorities, nor would they offend the great gentlemen in the Senate. Indeed, in law as well as in practice Constantine's church foundations, certainly in Rome and in the first half of his reign, were carefully set off from the public buildings both within the great show area and scattered all over town. Temples, administrative structures, theatres, thermae, triumphal arches, basilicas, circuses, and roads were *opera publica*. All over the Empire they were under the jurisdiction or at least the administration of the municipalities or the provincial governments. In Rome, the responsible municipal body was *Senatus populusque Romanus*, as represented by the Senate; and here, exceptionally, a piece of what one would expect to be imperial property, the palaces on the Palatine, was also counted among the *opera publica*. All other residences of the emperors belonged to the imperial patrimony, that enormous mass of real estate and other property which over the centuries by inheritance, purchase, and confiscation had accumulated in the hands of successive emperors, the *res privata*, the privy purse. In law, it was distinct from the *fiscus* which administered state property. In practice, by the fourth century the borderline was fluid and the emperor controlled both the fisc and the privy purse.[20] The terrains set aside by Constantine for his church foundations in and around Rome were, certainly in his early years, drawn from imperial estates, property controlled by the privy purse. They were in Constantine's free gift, as were the amounts needed for the construction of the churches and the vast estates, the income of which was to provide for their maintenance, *in servitio luminum* or *in redditum*. Both in fact and in law, then, the churches Constantine founded in Rome and in the first half of his reign were and would be in the eyes of the contemporaries his private donations. Only later, when the Church had been more fully integrated into a state viewed by Constantine as an *imperium Christianum*, and only far from Rome would he use for church foundations property of the fisc as well.[21]

The Lateran cathedral likewise should be seen within this framework. Constantine, as for his later church foundations in Rome, was careful to use for this, his first donation to the Christian community, property under his uncontested control. The mansion over which rose both the apse of the basilica and the baptistery behind presumably had been, like the other villas on that part of the Celian Hill, for some time in the hands of the privy purse, the *res privata*. The larger terrain where the nave of the basilica oversailed the barracks of the horse guards had obviously fallen, once the corps was cashiered, to the privy purse, as did, as a rule, confiscated property. Constantine could dispose of it as he pleased. He needed nobody's consent, as seventy years later the three founding emperors did when planning S. Paolo fuori le Mura; then, the city prefect in their name had to approach the Senate and People of Rome for permission to build across a minor country road, property by law of the *opera publica*. Nor did Constantine in planning the Lateran cathedral have to purchase or acquire by pressure private property, as he did for the thermae on the Quirinal. The Lateran basilica was his private foundation, financed from the privy purse and donated by him to the Christian community of Rome. Whether in the deed of gift the recipient named was the *corpus Christianorum Romae*, the *catholicae (ecclesiae) venerabile consilium*, or possibly the bishop matters little.[22] In any event it was, in 312–13 certainly, a legal body or an individual, set apart from any official institution, hence private by law. With this his first donation, I submit, Constantine set a precedent for his policy regarding church foundations, a policy which did not change until the mid-twenties, when the process of merging the Church into the State began in earnest. But by then Rome and her special problem lay behind him.

To preserve at least on paper the private and personal character of his church foundations seems to have been a basic principle of Constantine's building policy, in Rome anyhow. Size and splendor, shimmering marble pavements and wall revetments, gold mosaic and gilded ceilings (*fulgore corruscans aula*, said the inscription on Constantine's and Helena's gold cross at St. Peter's), a profusion of chandeliers and huge candlesticks in gold and silver—all produced the picture of ostentatious luxury which fourth-century men expected to see in a building erected by and for an emperor.[23] But, financed as they were by his private funds, the *res privata*, and handed over to the Church, a private legal body, Constantine's churches in Rome were in law private and, in any event, were nonpublic buildings set apart from the *opera publica*, public architecture in a proper sense. A sharp conflict emerges between the claims implied in plan, design, and furnishing of Constantine's church buildings in Rome and those implied by their remote location at the edge of or out of the city, as well as by their legal status as donations made from the property of the privy purse to a private legal body, as the Church was until the later years of Constantine's reign.

This conflict in fact was, it seems to me, built into and a crucial trait of Constantine's overall religious policies in the earlier years of his reign. From 312 to the mid-twenties it comes to the fore in Rome more markedly than elsewhere. Christ, Constantine was convinced, had granted him victory in the battle at the gates of Rome. In gratitude he was learning about and leaning toward the new faith.[24] He had made up his mind to protect and favor the Church and her faithful. But he meant to tread lightly, particularly in Rome. No good would come of hurting raw nerves. To be sure, large sections of the population of Rome and all through the West—though not as large a proportion as in the East—by 312–13 were Christians. But the leading strata of society, the Senate and the great families which in Rome wielded power, and with them many of the common people, stood aloof. With few exceptions, the aristocracy remained bound to the old traditions—to Rome's history, to her classical culture, to her religious beliefs. Individually, these great gentlemen, and for that matter anyone else, might, as many did, adhere to one of the new cults imported from the East—those of Isis, of the Great Mother, of Mithras, and of half a dozen others. They might believe, and most educated people did, in a Supreme Divinity, superior to all others, either unnamed or identified as the Invincible Sun God, *Sol Invictus*, ever since the latter part of the third century the emperor's Divine Companion, *Divus Comes Augusti*. As late as 310, Constantine was said to have recognized himself in the god's epiphany in the temple of the Sun in Autun as future ruler of the world. Indeed, until 325 the god appears on Constantinian coins, either as *Divus Comes*, joined to the emperor's portrait in profile, or by himself, standing or facing the emperor on the reverse (figs. 31 and 54).[25] Officially, nonetheless, the gods of the State, from Jupiter to the *genius populi Romani* and to the deified emperors, as well as their worship—priestly *collegia*, sacrifices, and all—had to be upheld. It was, if nothing else, a civic duty; the gods of Rome were the guarantors of the Empire's welfare, the *salus publica*. The great families of the city, as represented in the Senate, were in turn the guardians of the old civic and religious beliefs, of the worship of the gods and the maintenance of altars and temples.

Christianity was clearly incompatible with the old faith. It allowed for no gods aside from the One, and throughout the second and third centuries the refusal to sacrifice or to swear by any, including the emperor's, divinity had marked Christians as subversives unfit for public service; at best they could be tolerated provided they kept out of public life. Such attitudes, eroded by the end of the last persecution in 306, were obviously no longer feasible. By 312–13 even the most conservative supporter of the old order had to think of accommodation. Millions all over the Empire adhered to the new faith; it could not be repressed, as the failure of the final persecution had shown. The emperor, it was known, was moving towards Christianity: Christians were being promoted at court and in the administration; bishops in his retinue advised him on matters ecclesiastical and inevitably, one supposes, on occasion on matters temporal as well; as early as 312–13 the clergy was made exempt from public service and the heavy expense involved;[26] and everybody who had eyes could see how Constantine, starting in the fall of 312, poured funds into building churches and set aside huge estates to provide for their and the clergy's maintenance. Pagan leaders felt they had better avoid head-on clashes. The emperor, after all, was the emperor, and in composing an inscription or a panegyric one had best use a discreet formula, easily arrived at in a climate in which the concept of a nameless Supreme Deity was current among the upper strata: "The Divine Mind which deigns to reveal himself to you alone while leaving our care to minor gods"; "Highest Creator, who has as many names as there are tongues . . . force pervading all creation . . . power above all Heavens"; "that power, that majesty which distinguishes good and evil and ponders the weight of all merits"; "the Mind Divine which permeates the world, fused with all elements"; or, as on the Arch of Constantine, the victory "won by the inspiration of the deity and greatness of mind," an admirably vague formula arrived at, one suspects, by a bipartisan committee, Christians and gentiles, senators and courtiers, and designed to reconcile

31. Constantine and *Divus Comes*, gold solidus, 313

a gamut of religious feeling.[27] Whatever the phrasing, some formula like this was wanted so as to hurt neither pagan susceptibilities nor the emperor's; the more so since his religious beliefs and the degree to which he inclined towards Christianity were as vaguely known as, presumably, among pagans were the tenets of the new faith. After all, within the framework of political forces, the old families had every reason to seek accommodation with the victor; not only did he hold power, he had also come, as his propaganda stressed, as the liberator of Rome and the restorer of her old glory, just what they themselves strove for.

Like the pagans in the Senate and among the great Roman families, Constantine at the time of the conquest and for some time thereafter meant to tread lightly. The new faith versus the old one was not the question foremost in his mind. Certainly he was at that time anything but rigidly set against paganism; nor were his own religious beliefs by then firmly grounded. Roman emperor, that first and foremost he was; in 312–13 he would, I submit, have considered the state religion taboo, much as he might disagree with it. And precisely because he was emperor he would not have completely cut himself off from the bond to the Invincible Sun, his Divine Companion, nor would he have broken the tie to his own divine nature inherent in his imperial status. He had grown up at the court of Diocletian and had been bred in the tough tradition of the god-emperors of the tetrarchy, and there is no reason why he should have doubted his own divinity—neither in 312–13 nor, fundamentally deep down, ever. Nor did his contemporaries doubt it: the head of the colossal statue set up in 313 in the west apse of the basilica in Rome renamed after him was meant to strike with awe the mortals approaching the godhead (fig. 32)—a godhead blending severity, strength, and fairness rather than bludgeoning the faithful with fearsome brutality, as did the images of the tetrarchs (fig. 33), but still a godhead. The dream

32. Constantine, head of colossal statue

33. Heads of tetrarchs

before the battle at the Milvian Bridge had shown him the Chi-Rho, the monogram of Christ, the "sign of salvation." He had accepted it for himself and his army as an ἀλέξημα—a protective sign, a magic charm badly needed to combat the magic of the demons who fought for the enemy. A silver medallion struck in 315 shows Constantine wearing it as a badge on his helmet, presumably as he had done three years before at the conquest of Rome (fig. 34). A standard in the shape of the sign, golden and set with gems, the *labarum*, thereon became the φυλακ-τήριον, the talisman of the army. It clearly worked miracles, as Constantine himself told Eusebius after 324: the standard bearer was never touched by enemy arms, and wherever the *labarum* appeared, protected by its selected guard of fifty, the battle turned in Constantine's favor in all of his wars. It was the νικήτικον τροπαίον, the victory-bearing trophy, the secure guarantee of triumph. To Constantine the sign proved beyond any doubt Christ's boundless power, a power needed to overcome that of the old gods. For they, the demons, were by no means powerless. Through the sign he placed himself under Christ's protection, and in exchange, before knowing much about the new faith, he promoted Christ's cause and that of His Church. By the fall of 312 and still a year or two later, one gathers, his Christianity went little deeper. "The basis of the religious convictions of Constantine," to quote Alföldi, "was success on earth."[28]

Indeed, Constantine's was no sudden conversion, *pace* Eusebius' encomium or his own recollections, as told to his biographer twenty years later. Rather, to use a felicitous phrase of Ramsay McMullen's, one of many, he was groping his way "from the blurred edges of paganism to the blurred edges of Christianity."[29] Indeed, for another eight or nine

34. Constantine wearing
the Chi-Rho on helmet, silver medallion, 315

years he saw himself ruling fairly, or nearly so, over both pagans and
Christians. Whether as early as the fall of 312 he dropped from the ceremonial of the triumphal procession the protocollary reverence and sacrifice at the Temple of Jupiter on the Capitol—an act of defiance hard to
reconcile with his policy at that time—or whether that omission took
place first at the celebration of his decennalia in 315, starting in the
winter of 312–13 he distinctly and increasingly favored the new faith.[30]
But he tried to be, if not evenhanded, at least not openly antipagan, and
perhaps he was never as rabidly so as Eusebius would have us believe.
Even around 320 his attitude towards the "old superstition," the "ob-
solete practice," is still not hostility, but a somewhat comtemptuous tolerance. After all, half of his subjects, and more than half among the
leading circles, were pagan. Compromise, in the first decade of his reign,
anyhow, was a political must. The Sabbath law of 321, keeping Sunday
free of business, refers to the *dies solis* only, the day of *Sol Invictus* to
pagans—avoiding the Christian term by then traditional, *dies dominica*.
The prayer composed for the army in 324 in the war against Licinius
invokes an ill-defined Supreme Godhead—to hurt pagan sentiment among
officers and ranks would have been sheer folly. *Flamines* of the *gens Flavia*, Constantine's adopted ancestry, functioned in North Africa. As late
as the last decade of his reign, between 326 and 337, Constantine grants
permission to the town of Spello to set up a shrine for the *gens Flavia*
and to dedicate it to himself; albeit on condition that it not be polluted
fraudibus superstitionis—"by the magic arts of the Old Faith," one
would like to translate—that is, presumably, by sacrifices, whether animal or of incense. Nor did he ever abdicate title and office of the *pontifex maximus*; it may have been useful, anyhow, for controlling pagan
activities and acting as a supreme arbiter in the Church.[31] Constantine,
to be sure, grew ever closer to Christianity, and by the twenties, if not by

317, he was a Christian—as he understood it.[32] But having grown up in the old faith, he well understood pagan feelings and, into the twenties or even beyond, spared them, whenever warranted by the need to compromise or by his duty as Roman emperor to have the cult of the imperial family and of his own name continue.

More than elsewhere, forebearance with the old faith was needed in Rome. When he entered it in 312, certainly, and for quite some time to come Constantine had to find a modus vivendi with both the powers that so far had supported and continued to support him and those that ruled the city. The civil service and the officers' corps, overwhelmingly pagan, had served him well. In Rome the Senate and the great families, for some time on strained terms with Maxentius, were willing to cooperate. The population, suffering from famine and lacking welfare support, greeted the conqueror with shouts of joy as a savior and benefactor.[33] He could not afford to offend their feelings by forcing on them the new god who had given him victory. Perhaps he had gone too far already in the first flush of triumph in the days right after the conquest. Not only had he worn on his helmet and painted on the shields of his soldiers the magic sign of Christ, he had also set up in the midst of the city a trophy showing the Chi-Rho and in an inscription designated it as the talisman, the φυλακτήριον, of Roman rule and of the entire Empire. A golden or gilded statue of himself—perhaps as a god—dedicated to him in the same days by the Senate in the most frequented place of the city, presumably the Forum, he changed by placing in its hand the Chi-Rho and inscribed it to say that "through this Sign of Salvation, the true proof of bravery, [he] had liberated their city from the yoke of the tyrant and freed and restored to their old shining glory Senate and People of Rome." It was a challenge to non-Christians. Eusebius, as early as 316–17, knowing of it only by hearsay, sensed the provocation; would not pagan circles in Rome have understood as well and resented it? Certainly it was an imprudence, hastily indulged in by the victor. But if imprudence it was, Constantine made up for it by flattering the guardians of the Roman tradition in the very inscription placed on his statue. Official propaganda in these years consistently represented him as the defender of Roman liberty, the deliverer of the city, and the restorer of her ancient glory.[34] His image as propagated in these years—one need only think of the colossal head from the Basilica of Maxentius—is meant to recall past emperors, like Trajan, *princeps*, as it were, of the Senate.[35] The traditional institutions and the old families were consistently flattered. Coins honored Senate and *equites* and recalled the great past of Rome. On the very medallion of 315 on which Constantine wears the Chi-Rho badge on his helmet, his shield is adorned with the *lupa* suckling the twin founders of Rome. Avoiding confrontation with the conservative powers in Rome was an integral part of Constantine's policy in these early years. In fact, he strove to build up an alliance with the defenders of the old order.[36]

Only gradually did this policy change under the impact of his hardening Christian zeal and his concomitantly growing contempt for the old faith on one hand and pagan resentment on the other. Gentiles were bound to be offended, when upon entering Rome, be it in 312 or 315–16, he avoided the customary reverence to Jupiter on the Capitol. They were further offended when at his decennalia in 315 or 316 he refused to allow any sacrifices except those "without fire or smoke," thus excluding both animal sacrifices and the use of incense and admitting only either some vague deistic variant or Christian services. Still, despite the ever growing tension and his own ever stronger conviction of his obligations as a Christian, Constantine carefully refrained from offending gentile popular sentiment in Rome. Three decrees addressed to the Romans in 319 and 320 sharply illuminate his attitude. One, of February 1, 319, forbids under penalty of death at the stake admission of any haruspex to a private residence—he may have suspected black magic, and the demons after all were powerful. On May 15, 319, a second decree addressed to the people of Rome—this rather than the city prefect, an unusual procedure—upholds the previous injunction, but allows the consultation of priests and haruspices in public and the continuation altogether of services of the "Old Rite" for "those who believe this of use to themselves." Finally, a third decree, on December 17, 320, provides that haruspices are to be consulted in case the palaces on the Palatine or other public buildings, *opera publica*, are hit by lightning, to find out and report to the emperor the portent.[37] Clearly, Senate and People, upset by the first decree, insisted on the right to continue the accustomed ritual and procedure, and Constantine compromised to an amazing degree, notwithstanding his own religious beliefs, by then fully Christian. Prudence was the watchword in Rome.

Nor, in the years before the early twenties, would his Christian councillors have pushed the emperor too hard to battle in Rome more forcefully for their cause. Fanatics don't flourish at court. If left alone, the Majesty would come around in his own good time. The place of the Church vis-à-vis the State was ambiguous enough: protected by the emperor, loaded with gifts and privileges and recognized by imperial decree—that of Milan—but recognized by that very decree no more than other religions, and viewed askance and with suspicion by a majority of those in power in Rome. Christian leaders could not but feel uneasy in that bulwark of the old faith.

Ambiguity, then, underlies Constantine's Christian policy in Rome.

Ever since his victory at *saxa rubra* his faith, at first a shaky belief in Christ and His sign of victory, had grown firmer. His protection of the Church, open from the outset, increasingly expanded—witness his rescripts from 312 and 313 into the twenties favoring the clergy and permitting last wills in favor of the Church. He openly professed his beliefs in decrees and letters and, if the Speech to the Assembly of Saints really dates as early as 317, in long sermons both inside his palace and in public.[38] But he never did so in Rome. There he withheld his deepest convictions from public scrutiny. Conservative pagan circles could pretend not to know. Officially, the Majesty was just the emperor, a neutral arbiter. His religious beliefs, while openly confessed, were his private affair; for the Senate they need not exist. At his death in 337, Rome, still following old custom, raised him among the gods—only this can be the meaning of the painting displayed there which showed him above the vault of Heaven resting in his celestial abode.[39] It was a silent agreement of mutual knowledge, but not acknowledgment. Thus it complements the withdrawal into privacy which underlies the placing and the legal standing of Constantine's church foundations in Rome. Pagans would and did pretend these churches just were not there. None of them are mentioned by any of Constantine's pagan biographers—neither by Aurelius Victor, who succinctly lists his public buildings, nor by the Anonymous Valesianus, nor by Eutropius. Eusebius, who certainly would have listed and praised them to the skies, never was in Rome, and Constantine, strange to think, did not tell him. His churches in Rome were splendid; they were large; they were rooted in the soil of public building; and they therefore competed with and claimed by implication the rank of public architecture. But by law and in Constantine's own eyes they were not. Powerful though he was, he could not turn them legally into that—not in 312–13. No more could he make the Church into a public corporation at that point, even had he wanted to. Up to the early twenties in Rome, both Christianity and her monuments remained in an ambiguous position, claiming by implication but not by law official rank in the structure of the Empire.

From the twenties on, Constantine's religious policy changed. His beliefs had consolidated; he was a Christian. At the same time, he envisaged ever more clearly the potential of the Church as a unifying political tool in support of his domestic policies. Increasingly he thought of the Roman as a Christian empire.[40] Rome, held by the Senate and the old pagan families, resisted. Constantine had never been fond of Rome, visiting it but three times, in 312–13, in 315, and in 326, never for more than four months; the last visit ended in an open break with the city's powerful leadership. Rome obviously refused to become his Christian capital. Her rejectionist attitude, I submit, was one of the reasons, along with many others, political and strategic, which led Constantine to abandon Rome and the West altogether. In the East he would set up the Christian capital of his Christian empire: in Serdica-Sofia, in Thessalonikē, or, better still, in a city newly founded, unburdened by traditions and free of conservative opposition—in his own city, Constantinople.

II

CONSTANTINOPLE

Constantine had gone a long way from the Milvian Bridge to the victory on September 18, 324, at Chrysopolis over his co-emperor and rival Licinius.[1] Now he was the sole master of the Empire. Its administration and defense from Mesopotamia to Spain and from Africa to the Rhine and Britain were tightly organized with himself at the center. Unity, concord, was the watchword. His faith, too, had become firm; he *was* a Christian—as he understood it. The wars against Licinius, in retrospect at least, had become crusades against the forces of evil, embodied in the old faith. Christianity and the Church after 324 became solidly anchored in the State. No longer did Constantine view himself as a nearly even-handed ruler over Christians and pagans as he still had done around 320. Even before the final conflict with Licinius he had embarked on a holy war against paganism, and after Chrysopolis he increasingly saw himself as God's instrument, entrusted with the mission of spreading the faith and creating a homogeneous, Christian, and centrally ruled empire—one God, one Christ, "one empire on earth, set right."[2]

Such an empire required a permanent and Christian capital. It was cumbersome moving emperor, court, ministries, and high command every few weeks or months to another residence—from Trier to Vienne, to Arles, to Milan, to Serdica-Sofia, sometimes in the course of one year—as his predecessors and Constantine himself had done. It was also contrary to his guiding principle of unity. Pleas to rule from the old capital of the world could be of no avail. He had never taken to Rome, and despite his efforts to avoid friction with the ruling traditionalist group, mutual alienation had progressively grown. It culminated in 326 when at his vicennalia, more provokingly than on earlier occasions, he refused to appear on the Capitol for the solemn celebration and sacrifice to be performed.³ Political and strategic considerations favored a capital in the East, anyhow. During the years of tension with Licinius, 317 to 324, Constantine had ruled from one of the Balkan residences: Thessalonikē, Niš, Sirmium, Siscia, or Serdica-Sofia. But I very much doubt that he ever seriously thought of making any of these landlocked places his permanent capital; his ever-quoted statement, "Serdica is my Rome," means hardly more than "Where I am, is Rome."⁴ Certainly right after his final victory at Chrysopolis his mind was made up. Rather than use one of the older residences in the Balkans, he would lay out a new capital from scratch.

As its place he chose a promontory on the north shore of the Sea of Marmara, near the entrance to the Bosphorus, flanked to the east by a deep inlet, the Golden Horn. South, on the Asian shore, it faced Nicomedia, now Izmit, the favorite residence of Diocletian. A small Greek town, Byzantium, occupied the steep eastward tip of the promontory; founded a millennium before Constantine, it had been enlarged by Septimius Severus in A.D. 196. The site, molded by a number of hills, whether seven or not, was easy to defend. It dominated the Marmara and the straits, both the Dardanelles and the Bosphorus (fig. 35). Communications by land and sea were good. Port facilities could be improved. Two major roads started into Europe: westward the Via Egnatia to Thessalonikē and across northern Greece to Durazzo and Brindisi; northward and far more important by the fourth century the highway to Adrianople, Sofia, Niš, and the Danube provinces beyond, and thence to North Italy, the Rhineland, Gaul, and Britain. Across the Sea of Marmara a corresponding network of roads through Asia Minor linked up southeast with Ankara and Kaisarye in Cappadocia and beyond with Mesopotamia and the ever-threatened Persian frontier, south across the Taurus Mountains with the south coast of Asia Minor and with Syrian Antioch, Palestine, and Egypt, and east with Armenia (fig. 36). The site, then, was a nodal point on the map of the Empire, linking north and south, east and west. Finally, though that hardly weighed in Constantine's decision, it was and still is one of the most beautiful spots on earth.

Work on the new city went rapidly ahead. The *consecratio*, meaning possibly the tracing of the city wall, took place on Sunday, November 8, 324, barely six weeks after the battle at Chrysopolis.⁵ As in November 312, when founding the Roman cathedral, Constantine seems to have been in a hurry. In fact, just as the building of the Lateran was presumably in fulfillment of a vow for the victory at the Milvian Bridge, so the foundation and naming of Constantinople may well have been an ex-voto for the defeat of Licinius. This at least is suggested by a well-informed contemporary: "*Constantinopolim nuncupavit ob insignis victoriae memoriam. . . .*"[6] That Constantine himself, spear in hand, traced the line of the new walls seems plausible—such *sanctio* or *limitatio* was good old Roman custom, untainted by pagan connotations. So was the reported consultation of astrologers and augurs for a *dies faustus*—to any fourth-century mind except a Christian theologian's it was a matter of common sense; nor did Constantine apparently mind the cooperation of the τελέστης ("astrologer"?) Sopatros and the ἱεροφάντης Praetextatus, both well-known pagans. Construction must have been well under way by 326 if around that year ground could be broken for the cathedral.[7] The city walls appear to have been completed by 328, and this may have marked the *dedicatio*. At the same time a palace, one presumes, was made ready for the emperor, and on May 11, 330, the solemn consecration of the city, presided over by Constantine himself, took place in the new hippodrome; a coin showing the Tychē of the new city enthroned commemorated the occasion. Court and administration a few years before had already begun to establish themselves; a mint had started working by the summer of 326; and beginning in 330 the emperor spent at least a few months every year in his new capital.[8] By 334,

35. Constantinople, first half of seventeenth century

36. Road map, Roman Empire, Europe

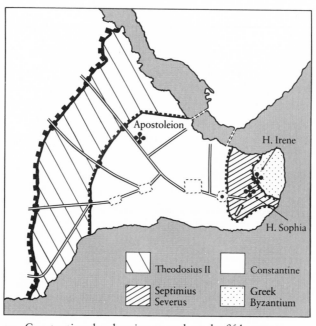

37. Constantinople, showing growth to the fifth century

it seems, the city was mapped out and the most essential structures—the walls, an aqueduct, streets, a palace, and administration buildings—functioned. Construction, to be sure, went on for a long time, and at Constantine's death in 337 only the sketch of a capital, to quote Dagron, existed. Large parts of the map were filled in only over the following century. But Κωνσταντινούπολις, Constantine's Own City, had been created.

It has been suggested that, notwithstanding the act of foundation in 324, not before 327 or 328 did Constantine decide to make the new city his capital. With all due respect to a great scholar and his interpretation of the numismatic evidence, I remain unconvinced. In 324, Constantinople already was not laid out like any of the dozens of other cities founded by previous or later emperors or by Constantine himself. Nor was it an imperial residence set up within an older town and provided with the imperial paraphernalia—palace, circus, huge thermae—such as the tetrarchic capitals Trier, Milan, Thessalonikē, and Nicomedia. Constantinople from the start was mapped out as a μεγίστη πόλις, a *Großstadt*. Laid out on a large scale both in overall plan and in detail, it covered roughly three square miles, almost four times the surface of the Severan town. The hippodrome was planned to seat fifty thousand, it seems. Altogether, the city was provided from the outset with the administrative apparatus to function as the capital of the Empire chosen by Constantine. *De facto* it was a new Rome, as later writers called it; *de iure* it was never meant to replace the old one on the Tiber. Rather, it was an alternative capital, a second Rome, equal but not superior to the old Rome, to quote Constantine's dedication decree. To hurt the pride of the old families and the Senate on the Tiber still would not do in 330.[9]

The new city necessarily was laid out within the framework of key elements extant: the site, the Greek town as enlarged by Septimius Severus, and the highways converging toward it from the west, north, and south. Greek Byzantium seems to have been no larger than Topkapu Saray, the sultan's palace compound at the tip of the promontory; but no remains have come to light (fig. 37). Nor are there many traces of the Roman enlargement, though it apparently quadrupled the surface of the Greek town; its protecting wall ran from the Sea of Marmara to a small harbor on the Golden Horn some 400 meters west of Greek Byzantium, and midway in the wall a gate (later known as the Old Gate) opened toward the Via Egnatia, into which the highway from the north had merged some 700 meters outside. The principal buildings of the Severan enlargement seem to have occupied the southwest sector: on the expanse in front of the Blue Mosque, Sultan Ahmet, where now Constantine's huge hippodrome is outlined, a first, presumably smaller, hippodrome; adjoining it to the north, the Baths of Zeuxippus, later enlarged by Constantine, small remains of which have been found; and still further north, a short distance south of H. Sophia, a porticoed square, the *tetrastōon*. There also would have been a few administrative buildings and a residence for a local magistrate, the provincial capital being Heraclea.[10] But everything is conjectural.

Whatever its layout, the Greco-Roman city became the starting point for Constantine's capital. The wall was pushed forward some 4 kilometers beyond that of Septimius Severus, and it ran a length of roughly 2.5 kilometers from the Sea of Marmara to the Golden Horn. Whether or not this wall already showed the fortification techniques displayed by that of Theodosius II built eighty years later another 4 kilometers further west with towers and *double enceinte*—still one of the great sights of the ancient world—is doubtful (fig. 38). More likely its pattern followed that of the Aurelian Walls of Rome (fig. 2). Inside Constantine's Wall, whatever its design, the old highways, the Egnatia starting from Severus' Old Gate and the north road branching off it, formed the main arteries of the new quarters between Severus's and Constantine's walls, obviously supplemented by transverse and parallel thoroughfares. Water was supplied by an aqueduct, built two hundred years before by Hadrian and perhaps repaired by Constantine. It fed at least the inner city, where the new palace rose; whether a second aqueduct was built by Constantine, as later Byzantine historians have it, remains open. Otherwise cisterns would have provided, as they did after the city was enlarged in the fifth century. Provisioning was secured. Shippers from eastern ports were exempted, as had been those from the West, from the burden of public services, the former with specific reference to their providing for Constantinople. A new harbor was laid out, though it was completed only after Constantine's death. Located on the Marmara coast rather than the Golden Horn, it allowed the heavy-bottomed grain ships from Alexandria to dock; nearby, the "Alexandrian warehouses" were built, to be supplemented later by the *horrea Theodosiana*. Everything was planned on a large scale, with an eye to the distant future, and was rapidly built. Obviously, more often than not construction was shoddy, as pagan and neo-pagan historians maintained. The population, to be sure, was lacking. But, by providing work and requiring services, the presence of the court and administration would attract labor, tradesmen, and hangers-on. To gather families of rank and substance, from Rome or elsewhere in the Empire, Constantine built elegant mansions and provided them with income from estates of the fisc, mostly in Asia Minor. Middle-class houseowners, landlords of tenements, and, one gathers, real-estate speculators would find advantageous the distribution of free bread attached, not to individuals or families, but to property. None of these plans took effect as fast as Constantine may have expected. But by 337, when he

38. Constantinople, Theodosian Walls, early fifth century

died, the population may have been as high as 90,000. Constantine's own city was alive, and it steadily grew.[11]

The old Greek town, within Constantine's master plan, was a mere anchor point. Inside, it remained untouched; its pagan shrines were left to decay; a Christian community center, close to the Greek Wall, was remodeled and enlarged by Constantine, but we don't know how. Named H. Eirene, Holy Peace, it continued to serve as cathedral until H. Sophia was completed in 360, and for some time afterwards the old H. Eirene and the splendid new H. Sophia jointly functioned as the cathedral. Only in 532, when it burned down in the Nika riot, was the old Eirene replaced by Justinian's church, as it stands, though remodeled in the eighth century.[12] The Roman part of the old town naturally became Constantine's government and palace quarter. Ever since it was laid out in A.D. 196, it had sheltered some of the representative splendor appropriate to such a function: the porticoed *tetrastōon*, a hippodrome, a large bath, some administrative buildings, and a double-storied, porticoed street—the *Regia*—leading from the Severan Old Gate to what became the entrance to Constantine's palace. Constantine's architects beautified, enlarged, or rebuilt on a grander scale these elements.[13] The porticoes of the *Regia* and the Zeuxippus Bath were filled with statuary, gathered from all over—"Dedicatur Constantinopolis omnium civitatum nuditate," says Jerome. The *tetrastōon*, enlarged, became the Augusteōn, a porticoed square and the focus of the government quarter; at its east

39. Constantinople, aerial view as of 1918. *Right foreground*, hippodrome and Blue Mosque (Sultan Ahmet); *left*, the palace site; *further left*, H. Sophia; *far left*, H. Eirene

40. Constantinople, hippodrome in fifteenth century(?), engraving, 1580

41. Constantinople, hippodrome, obelisk, base showing emperor enthroned in *kathisma*

end rose the Senate House, preceded by a colonnaded porch and embel-
lished with statues and reliefs, inside and out. But all this is known only
from literary sources and hence is conjectural in detail. The only Constantinian structure in that zone to survive is the circus, the hippodrome
(fig. 39). Its outline marked out in front of the Blue Mosque runs close to
450 meters in length and 120 meters in width, three-quarters the size of
the Circus Maximus in Rome. At the curved end, the *sphendonē*, the
arcaded substructures still rise 20 meters high from the slope; and while
the Egyptian obelisk on the *spina* was planted only under Theodosius I,
two generations after Constantine's death, and the second obelisk later
still, it was he who set up on the *spina* a row of ancient statuary and the
serpent tripod from Delphi. An engraving of late sixteenth-century date,
based, it seems, on a fifteenth-century drawing, shows further remains in
place: more objects on the *spina*; the *carceres* whence the competing
chariots started at the right, the northeastern end; and opposite, rising
from the substructures and enveloping the curved wall of the *sphendonē*,
a freestanding trabeated colonnade (fig. 40). Halfway down the length of
the racecourse, accessible from and part of the palace, rose the imperial
box, the *kathisma*, where Constantine on May 11, 330, presided over
the inauguration ceremonies for his new city, enthroned as was Theodosius sixty years later (fig. 41).[14]

Apparently, within Constantine's building program the hippodrome
received first priority, together with the construction of the city walls.
Not only was a circus, a hippodrome, integral to any imperial residence,
starting with the Circus Maximus in Rome at the foot of the palaces on
the Palatine, but since tetrarchic times a circus had gained new importance, for it was the place where the emperor encountered and showed
himself to the mass of his subjects, the people. The meeting between the
god emperor and the people, then, was a religious and State action. Constantine, while modifying the pagan elements of the ritual, nonetheless
retained the act proper. The hippodrome, being the site of the emperor's
epiphany, was the most important part of the palace quarter to be completed. Other buildings of the palace compound are known only from
descriptions, and they need not have been completed much before, if by
the time of, Constantine's death: the Daphnē palace with the audience
hall, the Magnaura, and the Banqueting Hall of the Nineteen Couches.
Only the overall site of Constantine's palace is known; of the structures,
only later additions of fifth- and sixth-century and later date have come
to light on the south slope of the hill. The Constantinian core seems to
have extended from the *kathisma* east and north to the end of the *Regia*,
near the Augusteōn Square (fig. 42).[15] There, the palace entrance rose,
sheltering the Bronze Gate. Above, a panel painting depicted Constantine
with the Chi-Rho, Christ's monogram, whether on his helmet or on a

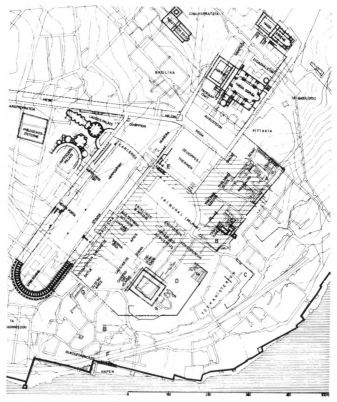

42. Constantinople, hippodrome and palace site, fourth century, plan

standard, and accompanied by his sons; spear in hand he pierced, so Eusebius interprets the picture, the Enemy in the guise of a sea monster; the picture may well be reflected in late fourth-century coins (fig. 43). Still, as the composition first appeared over the gate of Constantine's palace, the enemy may well have been mortal—the defeated Licinius— as was customary in late Roman numismatic iconography.[16]

A short distance north of the Augusteōn and south of the old Eirene church, Constantine laid out the new cathedral, later dedicated to Holy Wisdom, H. Sophia, and replaced in 532 by Justinian's grand structure. To this day, the domes of Justinian's building and at a short distance of H. Eirene, likewise rebuilt by him, dominate the eastward hill of the city (fig. 44). Constantine's H. Sophia, to be sure, was different in plan. But, like Justinian's, it would have risen over its surroundings. Like the hippodrome it was an integral part of the government area and almost an appendage to the adjoining imperial residence. Indeed, as did the imperial box at the hippodrome, it linked up with the palace by corridors and stairs to facilitate the emperor's solemn appearances. The situation of both emperor and Church had changed since, fourteen years before, the

43. Emperor subduing
monster, gold solidus,
365–75

44. Constantinople, view as of ca. 1930. *Background, left*, H. Eirene and *right*,
H. Sophia

Lateran cathedral was placed at the remotest spot in Rome. Begun, apparently, in 326 or thereabouts—not, as frequently stated, after Constantine's death—H. Sophia was consecrated only in 360. Damaged by fire in 404, it was reconsecrated eleven years later, but it burned to the ground in the Nika riot in 532. In its place, Justinian built his H. Sophia, that marvel of daring imagination and deficient statics which by a sheer miracle still rises aloft. Of the church consecrated in 415, a small section has come to light: a flight of stairs extending in front of the atrium and numbers of fragments belonging to a propylaeum, such as bases *in situ* (fig. 45), capitals, friezes, and segments of arches, coffered vaults, and pediments, all splendidly carved in the spirit of classical art reborn (fig. 46). The church to which they belonged must have been equally sumptuous, and it was huge: the atrium front (and hence, in all likelihood the church further east) measures over 66 meters in width, and, including the depth of the atrium, it cannot well have been shorter than 120 meters. In brief, it would have covered the surface of Justinian's church (fig. 47).[17] Inside, the sources tell us, the nave was flanked by aisles, presumably two on either side, supported by "amazing and miraculous" columns and surmounted by galleries. This plan, I submit, dates back to the early fourth century. Indeed, Constantine himself had financed the construction of just such a basilica—in Jerusalem, the martyrium on Golgotha east of Christ's Sepulchre in the Anastasis Rotunda. Eusebius has left a description, as always open to misinterpretation, and until the excavation, begun some years ago but immediately interrupted, is completed, the few surviving elements can only lead to questionable reconstructions, including those I have attempted in the past. However, we *do* know that, like the fifth-century H. Sophia, it was a basilica, with propylaeum, atrium, nave, four aisles, and galleries, albeit on a small

45. Constantinople, H. Sophia, fifth century, propylaeum, stairs and bases of colonnade

46. Constantinople, H. Sophia, fifth century, propylaeum, arch, detail

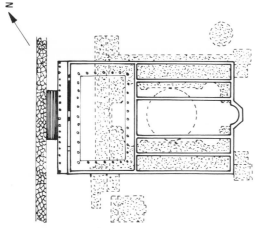

47. Constantinople, H. Sophia, fourth-century plan, hypothetical reconstruction overlaid on Justinian's church (stippled)

scale when compared with church foundations of Constantine's in Rome and, apparently, in Constantinople. A bread mold of seventh- or eighth-century date and a sixth-century mosaic map at Madaba render, if summarily, the sequence of structures in Jerusalem: a flight of stairs, a colonnaded propylaeum, an atrium, the martyrium-basilica, the rotunda of the Holy Sepulchre (figs. 48 and 50). Begun in 325–26, the structures were consecrated in 335, and it happens that the names and the origin of the two men in charge of construction are known: Zenobius, an architect and presumably a local man; and Eustathios, "presbyter from Constantinople," architect or administrator.[18] In the years from 325 to 335, as Constantinople was just being mapped out, his coming from there to Jerusalem means in all likelihood that he was an imperial emissary. Concomitantly, the pattern of the Jerusalem buildings—flight of stairs, propylaeum, double aisles, and galleries—is a *hapax legomenon* in the Holy Land. In Constantinople it remained common from the early fifth century on, if not before, as witness H. Sophia as rebuilt in 404–15, and from there it spread all over the Aegean coastlands: the Studios church in Constantinople and H. Demetrios in Thessalonikē are just two examples (fig. 49). Hence one may conjecture that the type was developed around 326 at Constantine's court in his new capital, and used in the very same years both by Eustathios at Jerusalem and, on a much grander scale, for the cathedral of Constantinople. This, the first H. Sophia, became the root from which the type spread. In short, I believe that the H. Sophia burned in 532 was actually Constantine's church, albeit repaired and redecorated in the early fifth century. The fire in 404 would have destroyed the roof and damaged the interior, but large parts of the

48. Bread mold, seventh to eighth century, showing Constantine's buildings at Holy Sepulchre, Jerusalem: *from left*, propylaeum(?) basilica, Anastasis Rotunda; *below*, interior of basilica(?) and paving of courtyard

49. Thessalonikē, H. Demetrios, interior

50. Madaba, mosaic map, sixth century, detail showing Jerusalem with colonnaded streets and, *center (upside down)*, churches on Golgotha

structure and certainly the plan would have remained; indeed, the front wall of the atrium behind the propylaeum of 415 may well be Constantine's. Also, a basilica of mammoth proportions such as the one that perished in 532 fits better than anything else the building mania of that colossal egocentric, Constantine.[19]

The construction of a church that size would obviously have taken time. But thirty-four years, from 326 to 360, seems excessive. Constantine could get things done in a hurry, as he showed at the Lateran and at St. Peter's in Rome. If work on H. Sophia, the cathedral, went so slowly, it means that he did not give it first priority in the building program for his new city. Other structures were of greater import—the palace, the hippodrome, and his forum and column, all finished by May 330.

The Forum of Constantine certainly was a key element in planning his city (fig. 37). Laid out in front of the Old Gate of the Severan town, it was the kingpin which linked Constantine's government area and palace in the old town to the new residential sectors extending north and west. From the Forum started the main arteries of the new quarters: the ancient Via Egnatia, called, inside Constantine's city walls, the Mese; and, branching off some 700 meters from the Forum, the street leading to the north gate, the Edirne Kapu or Adrianople Gate. At the branching-off point a square, the Philadelphion, sheltered, perhaps on column shafts, the groups of the tetrarchs now in Venice, whatever their place of origin. From the Philadelphion to the Forum the Mese was flanked by colonnaded porticoes, as was its older continuation, the Regia, leading from the Forum to the palace gate: street-colonnades, as for centuries had been customary in Hellenistic and late Roman city planning, witness Djemila in North Africa or, for that matter, Jerusalem as seen on the Madaba mosaic map (fig. 50). Constantine's Forum in his new capital occupied the crest of one of the hills, higher even than that on which rose palace, hippodrome, and H. Sophia. Circular or oval in plan, the Forum was enclosed by double-tiered colonnades and was linked both to the Mese and the Regia by arched passageways.[20] In general, then, it recalls circular piazze as known elsewhere in the Roman East. However, in contradistinction to such other piazze (that at Gerasa, for instance), Constantine's Forum was focused on a center column; this, Constantine's Column, was its true raison d'être. Badly damaged in a fire—hence its name, the Burned Column, the column survives, provided in 1701 with an ungainly socle and base, 2.35 meters above the old forum level (fig. 51). The shaft, roughly 25 meters high, 2.90 meters in diameter, and composed of nine porphyry drums, originally rested with its base on a tall socle, 5 meters high and enclosed in a vaulted and arched *tetrapylon* raised on five steps—a sanctuary, the sources suggest, enclosing an altar for celebrating Mass (fig. 52). Atop the column stood a bronze statue of

Constantine, transformed, so the sources say, from one of Helios by substituting Constantine's head for that of the god; nonetheless, the Sun God's seven rays still radiated from the emperor's head. His left hand held a lance, his right a globe, surmounted in all likelihood by a Tychē—the latter a symbol of the city's good fortune rather than a goddess. A small representation of column and statue as hallmark of Constantinople appears on the *Tabula Peutingeriana*, a reliable thirteenth-century copy of a second-century map as revised in the fifth century—in its main features it coincides with the descriptions given by early Byzantine sources, except that under the hands of the copyists the globe has turned into a wreath (fig. 53). The resemblance to figures of Helios on both third-century and still later Constantinian coins—rays, lance, globe, and all— is obvious (fig. 54).[21]

What the new quarters beyond the Forum of Constantine looked like remains, to all practical intent, unknown. The mansions, provided for wealthy settlers, may have resembled those of fifth- and sixth-century date known from Antioch. Whether they were loosely scattered or built close to one another is conjectural. Middle- and lower-class housing presumably was left to private initiative (read, more often than not, building speculation): multifamily dwellings, two and more stories high; single-family houses; hovels of all descriptions; or mansions with rent-producing shops along the street. How much of such diversified housing had gone up by the time Constantine died remains an open question. It grew rapidly in the century from 350 to 450. But as early as the second half of the fourth century, numerous estates of great gentlemen spread in the suburbs outside Constantine's Wall, presumably interspersed with middle-class housing, and by 412 these suburbs had become so heavily populated as to require the construction, ca. 1.5 kilometers further west, of the new Theodosian Wall. The inner city, covering the surface of the Greek, Roman, and Constantinian town, was so overbuilt as to need zoning regulations by 450, forbidding housing more than ten stories high. Under Constantine that day was still far off. His "sketch of a city" at best outlined the map of the future, tracing streets and building lots and preparing or providing essential utilitarian construction. To be sure, Constantine apparently also planned to satisfy the spiritual needs of a Christian population, expected to grow rapidly, by founding churches as the need arose. In the early thirties he commissioned fifty Bibles to be written for churches to be built in his new city—obviously as a reserve. But Eusebius is suspiciously vague in naming any church begun or completed by 335 or 337 which he could have seen when in Constantinople—except one.[22]

In fact, only one church was both begun and completed by Constantine in his very own city: his mausoleum church, the Holy Apostles. Planted

51. Constantinople, Column of Constantine as of ca. 1880–90

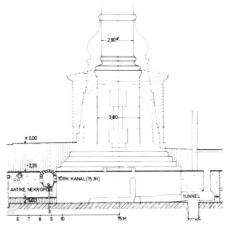

52. Constantinople, Column of Constantine, socle, reconstruction

53. *Constantinopolis*, personified, with Constantine's Column, *Tabula Peutingeriana*, detail

54. Helios, coin

on the highest point of the area inside the Constantinian Walls (fig. 37) and close to them near the Adrianople Gate, it was complete when the emperor was buried inside it in May or June 337, Eusebius apparently being an eye witness. Justinian replaced it by a new structure; consecrated in 550, it was remodeled several times over in the following centuries—S. Marco in Venice and a number of miniatures in Byzantine manuscripts seem to reflect it as it stood in the twelfth century. Between 1461 and 1473 it gave way to a mosque, the Fatih of Mehmet II; remodeled so thoroughly, from 1761 to 1771, as to amount to a rebuilding on a monumental scale, the Fatih to this day dominates the city and its skyline, as presumably did the Apostle church of Justinian and, earlier, that of Constantine (fig. 55).[23] In fact, by the site chosen Constantine's mausoleum church already made unusual claims. Rising inside the city walls at the farthest point from the palace, it defied both the ancient Roman taboo against burial within the city limits and the recent tetrarchic custom of placing the emperor's mausoleum inside the palace precinct, as witness Spalato or Thessalonikē. Only one example of a siting similar to Constantine's comes readily to mind: the mausoleum of Augustus in Rome, erected outside the "Servian" city but enclosed by and close to the later Aurelian Walls, far from the palaces on the Palatine.

Eusebius' *Life of Constantine* appears to be the only source from which to envisage Constantine's church and the surrounding buildings.[24] The church, from his account, rose within a large courtyard, enveloped by colonnaded porticoes, to which were attached exedrae, fountains and guardhouses, large thermae, and imperial living quarters, οἶκοι βασίλειοι. Whether many of these appendages by 337 were still in the planning stage, as is likely, matters little. The thermae, the Κωνσταντινιάναι, apparently were built only after 345.[25] The church, though, was ready for Constantine's funeral in 337.[26] A reference in a poem by Gregory of Nazianz to its cross shape, presumably with arms of equal or nearly equal length, is corroborated by filiations of the plan; the late fourth-century Apostle church in Milan, now incorporated in the Romanesque church of S. Nazaro (see below, fig. 71), a nearly contemporary church excavated at Antioch-Kaoussié, and a fifth-century church at Gerasa in Jordan are but a few examples (figs. 56 and 57). Whether in Constantine's Apostle church the arms were aisleless as at Antioch or divided into nave and aisles as at Gerasa remains open. Eusebius only says that the church was "of indescribable height," that the walls inside were sheathed with colored marble, and that the ceilings were coffered and gilded.[27] Outside, the roof shone with gilded bronze tiles, and a δωμάτιον, "a little house," enclosed by bronze grills rose, Eusebius says, from the roof. If so, it would presumably have surmounted the crossing.

But, given the notorious imprecision of Eusebius' architectural descriptions, one wonders whether by chance this δωμάτιον or another one rose inside in the center of the church over the catafalque: an οἶκος, as later writers seem to refer to it, a canopy inside the enclosed altar site and flanked by twelve "sacred στῆλαι" commemorating the apostles—cenotaphs, honorific pillars, inscribed plaques, whatever the meaning—

55. Constantinople, Fatih mosque from the northwest

on either side.[28] Moreover, Eusebius says, Constantine had arranged for
Mass to be celebrated near or over his tomb. Thus, to quote verbatim,
"this thrice-blessed soul is glorified jointly with the greetings addressed
to the apostles and it is a place of gathering for God's People and worthy
of divine service and the celebration of Mass." The arrangements willed
by Constantine were, to put it mildly, extraordinary. To orthodox Christians they were shocking; so much so that in 359 his son Constantius
had the sarcophagus removed, first to H. Akakios. Later it was brought
to the mausoleum rotunda which Constantius began to build, attached
to yet separate from the Holy Apostles.[29]

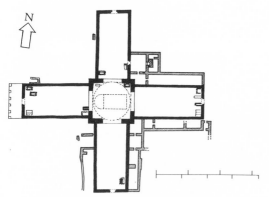

56. Antioch-Kaoussié, St. Babylas, plan

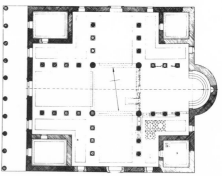

57. Gerasa, Church of the Apostles, Prophets,
and Martyrs, 464–65, plan

The palace where Constantine resided and the hippodrome where he
appeared to his subjects, the Forum where on the column his statue rose
high over the city, the Apostle church and his catafalque—all mark the
city as his: Κωνσταντινούπολις, the πόλις ἐπώνυμος, the second Rome,
alternate capital of the world, with the hallmarks pertaining to the one
on the Tiber—seven hills, if hard to list; palace and hippodrome, as
on and below the Palatine; Forum and column, like Trajan's; an imperial mausoleum within the walls, like that of Augustus, Rome's second
founder. Yet, to Constantine his very own city was neither the dream of
an egomaniac nor an *imitatio Romae* pure and simple. She was, I submit,
an ex-voto offering to Christ, who had given him victory over Licinius
and with it the rule over the Empire. What he saw in the city "on which
on God's behest I have bestowed forever my own name" interlocks with
his thanksgiving to Christ and with his many-faceted understanding at
that point in his life of Christianity, his place within it, and his special
relation qua emperor to Christ.[30]

Clearly, Constantine's city was not the Christian capital Eusebius would
have liked to see. The cult of traditional pagan deities, their shrines and

festivals, to be sure, Constantine seems to have left in the old city to decay slowly, not admitting them to the new city quarters. Zeus, Hera, and the rest of Olympus were dead, after all. A shrine of the Tychē—not a deity, she—was allowed to survive, or was even newly built; so allegedly was one of Rhea of immemorable age, but her statue was changed into the figure of an *orans*, although these are stories told by a latter-day neo-pagan antiquarian.[31] Certainly, the statues of the old gods and their mementos collected from all over were set up by Constantine—neither out of reverence nor, as Eusebius has it, for ridicule[32]—they just belonged to the decor of any late antique city and certainly to that of the second Rome.[33] On the other hand, Eusebius's tale of Constantine's placing "in the forum"—his own?—groups of the Good Shepherd and of Daniel and the lions smacks of Christian reinterpretation. The painting over the palace gate, Constantine piercing an enemy, likewise could have referred to his victory over Licinius, rather than *the* Enemy, though the second meaning may have been subintended. More clearly than elsewhere, the embarrassment of Eusebius in trying to present Constantinople as the Christian capital which he would have liked it to be becomes obvious in the intentional vagueness of his references to churches built by the emperor in his capital. "The city that bears his name he caused to shine with many sanctuaries and with very large martyrs' shrines and with the most beautiful houses both in the suburbs and within. . . ." is a statement so general as to amount to an evasion: either the churches were barely begun, like H. Sophia; or they were insignificant shrines and community centers, like H. Eirene, remodeled under Constantine; or they were in the planning stage. By the time Eusebius last visited Constantinople, presumably at the time of Constantine's funeral in 337, apparently no church was completed, except the Apostle church.[34]

No ordinary Christian capital, then, this Constantine's Very Own City—for that it was, first and foremost. One only need view the places where and the monuments in which Constantine reveals himself to his subjects on the Bosphorus. From the palace, to paraphrase Eusebius—at the eastern tip of Constantinople, one ought to remember—he comes forth at sunrise to let shine, as if simultaneously with the light of the sky, the rays of his generosity on all who approach him, just as the sun, Helios, sheds on all the globe the radiance of his glow. His epiphany as Helios comes to the fore with even greater force both in his portrait statue atop the column in his Forum and in the rites established by himself for the consecration of the city in the hippodrome on May 11, 330, and continued into the sixth century.[35] Descending the winding stairs from his apartments and enthroned in the *kathisma*, the imperial box, Constantine presided over the games, greeted by the ritual acclamations of the crowd. In a variation on the age-old custom of carrying on a char-

iot in the religious procession opening the circus games the statue of the
emperor among those of the gods,[36] a gilded wooden statue of Constantine rode into the arena, flanked by soldiers in parade uniform carrying candles. Rather than an ordinary portrait, however, the statue was a
copy of that on the column, Constantine as Helios. After making the
round of the arena, the chariot stopped opposite the *kathisma* and, so
Constantine willed, the then ruling emperor was to make *proskynesis*
before the image. The ritual continued far into the sixth century—καὶ
νῦν, says Malalas[37]—revealing Constantine as on May 11, 330, he had
revealed himself to his subjects: in the guise of the Sun God, riding on
the sun chariot and carrying in his hand the Tychē of Constantinople as
the divine founder of the city on which at Christ's behest he had bestowed his own name—a strange contradiction, indeed.

Equally strange is what is known of the ceremonies at the column on
the Forum, surmounted by the bronze colossus of Helios bearing Constantine's features. On an altar inside the tetrapylon which enclosed socle
and base of the column, Mass was celebrated, lamps were lit, incense was
burned, and prayers and supplications were offered "to Constantine's
image on the column . . . as if to God to avert disasters," or so an outraged Photius interpreted the report of Philostorgius, who as late as the
turn of the fourth century witnessed the ritual. Seen through the eyes of
a ninth-century patriarch, the rites were outrageous indeed. Popular superstition and emotion, seventy years after Constantine, had swamped
the liturgical elements of a regular service; to the Christian masses, the
founder of their city had become its tutelar divinity. "The goings-on at
the catafalque and at the column," as a fifth-century eyewitness called
them, continued for a long time, and as late as 533, when an earthquake
shook Constantinople, the people streamed to the Forum, "with supplications and prayers and watching through the night."[38] No regular
service is mentioned; rather it was by then an aliturgical *statio*, a gathering of the faithful without benefit of clergy. On the other hand, in the
late twenties or in 330, the Christian consecration service for the city
may well have taken place at the foot of the column. Theophanes ex-
pressly states that the column marked "the very spot where Constantine
ordered the city to be built," as indeed it is there that the new quarters
were hinged to the old sectors; Malalas refers to the celebration of Mass
at the consecration ceremonies while describing Forum and column in his
periegesis through the city. Finally, an eighth-century text, if it can be
trusted, tells of the statue being placed atop the column accompanied by
a service, the priest offering a prayer and the people chanting the Kyrie.[39]

Constantine certainly meant his statue to rise high over his capital,
shining forth to his people like Helios. For centuries Hellenistic rulers
and Roman emperors had usurped for their portraits on coins the radiat-

ing crown of the Sun God, and for a generation or more prior to Constantine the Invincible Sun, *Sol Invictus*, had been the Roman emperor's Divine Companion, his heavenly protector and double. Thus, emperor and Sun God appear on coins, profiles overlapping; they are, as Kantorowicz phrased it, interchangeable magnitudes. Far into Constantine's time solar imagery permeates official rhetoric and coinage: as late as 313 the Sun God appears as the Divine Companion of Constantine in the traditional double portrait (fig. 31). By himself the god is not dropped from Constantine's coins before 325 (fig. 54), and in the late twenties or the thirties in a well-known inscription the citizens of Termessos in Asia Minor still address Constantine as the New Helios, the New Sun.[40] Of course, if we imagine ἥλιος written lowercase, the pagan connotation disappears. The Sun remained an interchangeable likeness, a τύπος of the Christian as it had been of the pagan Roman emperor, and Eusebius never ceases to shower on Constantine the features and epithets proper to the sun: from his palace he issues forth like the sun at dawn; at Nicaea he enters, "a heavenly messenger of the Lord, shining as with rays of light, glowing with the fiery radiance of a purple robe and adorned with the gleaming transparency of precious stones"; and, in Heaven after death, he is "resplendent in a brilliant garment of light."[41] Who could help thinking of the shining glory of the Lord?

However, the trouble lay right there. Constantine felt no qualms about manifesting himself as Helios. More orthodox Christians would bridle at the idea; not so much or not only for its pagan, but for its Christian implications. Had not the features of the Sun God ever since the third century been fused into the figure of Christ? He was the New Sun, addressed just as Constantine had been by the citizens of Termessos; He was the Sun of Justice, the Sun of Salvation, the Rising Sun, the One from the East.[42] He rose in the chariot of Helios, seven rays shooting from his halo, as in a mosaic on the vault of a small mausoleum below St. Peter's in Rome, buried when the foundations of the basilica were laid around 322 (fig. 58).[43] This very merger of Helios into Christ would have made scandalous, I suspect, to strict Christians the epiphany of Constantine as Helios and the celebration of Christian services at the column. Eusebius in his rhetorical imagery had gone to the very limit in bestowing on Constantine the attributes of the Sun. The further equation with Helios and implicitly with Christ went beyond what he considered possible for a Christian. Hence, I suggest, his silence regarding column, statue, and services and the obvious disapproval of late fourth- and fifth-century writers.

Within Constantine's understanding of Christianity, on the other hand, his own epiphany as Helios and the implied link to Christ seem in no way extraordinary. Nor did he apparently feel disturbed by the provisions he had made for his burial in the Apostle church: his catafalque's being flanked by the twelve στῆλαι, quasi-images of the disciples, to whom he thus implicitly claimed superior rank; his commanding Mass to be celebrated forever over or near his sarcophagus; the gathering of the faithful to worship at his mortal remains; and the buildings planned or erected around his burial church—the precinct laid out to hold large crowds, the baths for the convenience of those come from afar, and the palace, presumably for visits by future emperors. All was designed to make his resting place the center of continued veneration and the goal of pilgrimages. Contemporaries, as well as later generations, could hardly fail to think of another sepulchre which he had had his architects lay out a decade before: Christ's on Golgotha. There, too, the tomb was surmounted by a canopy, an οἶκος or δωμάτιον, supported by twelve columns arranged in pairs (fig. 59); there, too, it was enclosed, if not under Constantine, then shortly later, in a commemorative structure, the Anastasis Rotunda, as its focus and raison d'être; and there, too, provision had been made for continued veneration and for pilgrimages.[44]

Constantine's portraiture in the guise of Helios, the consecration ceremonies of Constantinople in the hippodrome and the services at his column, the arrangements he willed for his burial place in the Apostle church—all seem today odd ways for the first Christian emperor to manifest himself to the people whom he wanted to lead to Christ. Starting with Eusebius and continuing to this day, theologians and historians have tried desperately to explain away what they considered embarrassing. The placing of the tomb and its veneration have been defended as reconcilable with Christian custom: Constantine merely wanted to share in the prayers addressed to the apostles; he saw himself as one of them and their leader.[45] Or else both the situation in the Apostle church and the Helios-Constantine statue have been interpreted as survivals of paganism, harmless in themselves: the apostles with their leader revived the Thirteen Gods venerated in Lycia, and thus guaranteed Constantine's place among the gods;[46] or Constantine by family tradition and early religious experience was so firmly rooted in the sun cult that he felt quite natural his continued veneration of and identification with the Sun God, "symbol of the dynasty," even after his conversion.[47] The ceremonies in the hippodrome have been interpreted as but a reversion to the ruler cult. Rarely has the resemblance between Constantine's own and Christ's burial places and his resulting claim, first pointed out by Heisenberg[48] (and branded as a monstrosity),[49] been carried to its conclusion: that Constantine viewed himself as an earthly manifestation of Christ, comparable to Him, albeit within the limits of the *condition humaine*.

Certainly this is contrary to Christian belief as commonly understood and shocking to many in their picture of the first Christian emperor. To

58. Rome, St. Peter's, Mausoleum of Julii, mosaic showing Christ as Helios

60. Constantine's consecration coin, showing him rising to heaven

59. Ampulla, detail showing canopy over Holy Sepulchre

Constantine it in no way deviated from Christianity. He was by 330 a firm Christian, profoundly religious and deeply conscious of his mission as a Christian emperor to lead the world to God. But precisely because he was the first Christian emperor, his Christianity was bound to have a note of its own. The place held within a Christian universe by a Christian emperor was crucial. An emperor by definition was a god. Constantine, deeply imbued with the responsibilities and prerogatives of his imperial position and mission, was not yet ready to abdicate his inherent divinity in favor of a "by the grace of God," as would the next generation on the throne, born and brought up as Christians. He had to fit his godhead as best he could into a scheme of the universe in which only the One God could exist.[50] This was possible for him within the framework of political theologies both inherited and developed by court theologians such as Eusebius: the concept, deeply rooted in the Hellenistic tradition, of the ruler and the god being linked to one another in a particular and personal interaction. The god had taken his abode in the king; or the Invincible Sun, *Sol Invictus*, and the emperor were interchangeable magnitudes, the god being the emperor's double and heavenly protector. Just so, one suspects, Constantine would have seen Christ not only as the ruler of all mankind, but also as his very own godhead. To Him he stood in a highly personal relationship, almost as his pagan panegyrist twenty years before had phrased it, "The Divine Mind who to you alone deigns to reveal himself." Christ was, as it were, another *comes divinus* who guided all his steps—"quod duce te mundus surrexit in astra triumphans // hanc Constantinus victor tibi condidit aulam"—so the inscription on the triumphal arch of Old St. Peter's.[51] Constantine was the φίλος θεοῦ, the favorite—this rather than the friend—of God, singled out and taken personally under His wing. Concomitantly, he would have seen himself as an earthly double of Christ, tied to and responsible to Him in an intimate personal relationship.

Such views, needless to say, are embedded in the concepts which underlie the political theology of Constantine, as presented by Eusebius and brilliantly interpreted in our time by Baynes, Peterson, and Ladner:[52] the Christian Empire is but an imitation, a *mimesis*, and concomitantly a forecast of the Heavenly Kingdom. Constantine has been chosen to envisage the image of the kingdom beyond and to shape its reflection on earth.[53] Thus he himself is an image of Christ: an image, no more; he angrily rebukes a bishop for flattering him by saying that after death he would rule in Heaven jointly with Christ. That was blasphemy. What he had in mind was far from such συμβασιλεία. Christ and he were not interchangeable magnitudes. But they were parallel figures. Christ the Logos ruled in Heaven as the Father's regent, his ὑπάρχος. From there He guided the emperor's policies and his every step. Thus divinely guided from above, Constantine ruled below as a regent, a ὑπάρχος of the God-head with the mission of leading the world to Christianity and thus of creating on earth an imitation of the Kingdom of Heaven.

Being impervious to theological niceties, Constantine never defined the precise relationship. What mattered was that on earth in the context of politics and rulership the first Christian emperor stood for Christ. His epiphany as Helios, the Sun of Salvation, on his column would have appeared to him as natural as the celebration there of Mass; so would the *proskynesis* before a copy of that image in the hippodrome; so would, finally, the placing of his sarcophagus amidst and superior to the apostle στῆλαι, its continued Christian veneration, and the undeniable resemblance of its arrangements to those of the Sepulchre of Christ in Jerusalem.

Following age-old custom at an emperor's death, a coin was struck in 337 to commemorate Constantine's *consecratio*, his being raised to the gods—strange, it would seem, in the case of the first Christian emperor, but not so much strange as testifying to his not quite having renounced his divinity. Even Eusebius thought it quite normal and described the coin in detail.[54] The obverse shows Constantine, the toga draped over his head, the Roman gesture traditional when approaching the godhead for sacrifice or prayer and contrary to Christian custom. On the reverse the customary *consecratio* scene is presented in a *re-interpretatio Christiana* (fig. 60). Traditionally the defunct emperor, clad or naked, was shown standing on the sun chariot placed atop the funeral pyre and surrounded by other pagan features.[55] On Constantine's coin, instead, pyre and all pagan reminiscences are omitted and the emperor, draped in a shroud, on a quadriga gallops heavenward towards the extended hand of God. Inevitably the ascension of Elijah on a fiery chariot comes to mind[56]—of Elijah, who, so Cyril of Jerusalem says, was carried up *as if* to Heaven, rather than ascending there outright as did Christ.[57] Whatever the defunct Majesty might have wanted to see on his *consecratio* coin, his sons' theological advisers reduced Constantine's claims as stated all too clearly in his burial arrangements to a level defensible by more orthodox Christians. Even so, his privileged position, high above all other mortals, was acknowledged: for who aside from Elijah (and Helios) had been taken up straight as if to Heaven?

No document of Constantine's time appears to speak of his city as the Christian capital as opposed to the old one, Rome. But the monuments do—the three focal points on the map of the city as laid out by Constantine: the palace and the hippodrome, the Forum and Constantine's Column, the Apostle church and his catafalque.

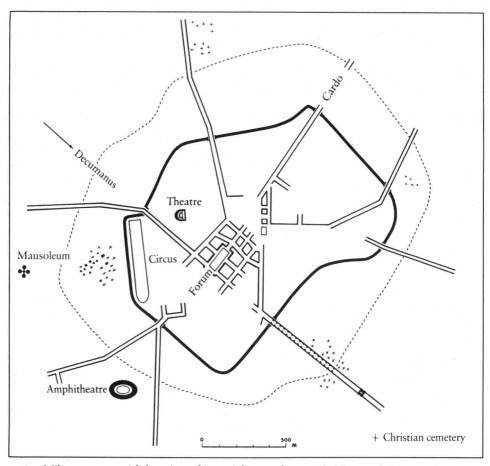

61. Milan ca. 300, with location of imperial mausoleum at S. Vittore al Corpo and cemeteries (stippled)

III

MILAN

The map of Milan in the second half of the fourth century mirrors a conflict of political and religious ideas, just as that of Rome did fifty years before under Constantine, with the difference that in Milan the contenders were Christian factions and bishop versus emperor rather than an emperor turning to Christianity versus a conservative pagan senate.

Until the last decade of the third century, Milan was a respectable county seat, a commercial and administrative center among similar towns all over the Empire (fig. 61).[1] It had its city wall, forum, theatre, well-appointed mansions, warehouses, and, pretty far out, an amphitheater with as many as thirty thousand seats. Maximian Herculius, Diocletian's co-emperor, between 293 and 305 made it his residence. Situated on the crossroads of the great east-west and north-south highways from the Balkans to Gaul and from Africa and Rome to the Alpine passes and the Rhineland, it was strategically located both to counter the increasing threats from the barbarians across the Rhine and the Tweed and to maintain communications between the eastern and western halves of the Empire (fig. 36). Hence, around A.D. 300 the town was enlarged towards the northeast and provided with new walls, a large bath, the thermae Herculianae, a circus at the southern edge of town, and a palace located presumably nearby. Outside town, along the road to Rome, the street for a mile's length was flanked by colonnaded porticoes, and, as in Thessalonikē and in other imperial capitals in the East, the colonnades began at a tetrapylon recalling the Arch of Galerius at Thessalonikē or the Janus Quadrifrons in Rome.[2] Likewise out of town as custom required and inside a fortified precinct, Maximian built his mausoleum. It was drawn by a Netherlandish draughtsman, the Anonymous Fabriczy, around 1570 as it stood alongside the Romanesque church of S. Vittore al Corpo, shortly before being incorporated into the late sixteenth-century rebuilding of that church (fig. 62). Like the Romanesque church and its rebuilding, the mausoleum remains known only from that *veduta*, and from plans, descriptions, and a partial excavation: a large steep octagon, with small windows, the top wall lightened by a dwarf gallery, the inside with alternately rectangular and semicircular niches, sheathed with colorful marble and sheltering the emperor's porphyry sarcophagus.[3]

It seems only natural that after Constantine's death the Augusti ruling the western part of the Empire should make Milan their capital—a semipermanent capital, for threats on the frontiers or from usurpers or co-emperors and the need to administer in person their far-flung provinces forced them to be always on the move to other equally semipermanent capitals: Aquileia, Sirmium, Vienne, Trier. None could claim to be a capital in the sense Rome or Constantinople was—a *caput mundi* either through its glorious past or through having been founded by the great Constantine as an alternate Rome. Still, Milan was conspicuous among imperial residences in the fourth century. Ausonius around 385 in his *Ordo urbium nobilium* ranked it seventh among the cities of the Empire

62. Milan, S. Vittore al Corpo and adjoining mausoleum, drawing, ca. 1570

and glorified it for its riches and the splendor of its buildings—the "numberless elegant mansions," the double fortification, the enlargement of the town, the circus, the theatre, the churches (*templa*), the palace, the mint, the Thermae Herculianae, "large like a city quarter [*regio*]," and the colonnades (*peristylia*), perhaps colonnaded streets, filled with sculptures (*signa*). Its strategic importance had grown, if anything. The population, whether or not as high as 130,000 to 150,000, seems to have spilled over into suburbs along the highways to Rome, Pavia, Vercelli, Como, and Verona. The nearly unbroken presence of the emperors from Constans and Constantius II to Theodosius I, ever returning there from campaigns and administrative forays, made the city between 340 and 402 the principal seat of imperial power in the western half of the *orbis Romanus*.[4]

Inevitably, therefore, Milan also came to hold a key position in the politico-theological wars between orthodox and "Arians," fought out bitterly from roughly 340 to 390 by bishops, congregations, and emperors and their families and courts.[5] As for the terms *orthodox* and *Arian*, the first, of course, covered a number of variations on the concept of Christ's being consubstantial with the Father, as laid down in the Nicene Creed and staunchly upheld by Athanasius of Alexandria; the second, a gamut of shadings on that of His being similar to the Father, as maintained by Arius and his faction—*homoiousios* rather than *homoousios*, in Greek. The iota made all the difference, and the term *Arian* was used as a pejorative by the opponents as loosely as the expressions *Reds* or *Fascists* are in our time. I, for one, would rather speak of Nicenes and anti-Nicenes. The former were primarily the Egyptian followers of Athanasius and almost as a body the Western episcopate, clergy, and congregations; the anti-Nicenes were, roughly speaking, Easterners. Both parties appealed for support to the emperors, first to Constans, then to Constantius II, and the fight thus focused on their residence, Milan.

Constantius, at first favorable to the Nicenes but understandably incensed at Athanasius for having negotiated with the counter-emperor Magnentius, sided with the anti-Nicenes. Once he was firmly established in 353, he exerted all possible pressure to have the Western bishops accept an "Arianizing" creed. At a synod, held in Milan in 355, a corresponding formula was forced through against the resistance of the Italian and Gallic episcopate and, apparently, a large pro-Nicene sector of the local congregation. In the end the leading recalcitrant bishops were arrested in the cathedral and exiled—among them Dionysius of Milan, Liberius of Rome, and Lucifer of Cagliari—and the meetings of the synod were moved from the cathedral to the palace, probably so as to exclude the vociferous Nicene faction among the congregation.[6] To replace bishop Dionysius, the emperor's choice fell on an anti-Nicene Cappadocian, Auxentius. The emperor was firm, and, like his father Constantine, he was widely accepted as arbiter in matters ecclesiastical and as *de facto* head of the Church. Under continued pressure and resistance, two synods in 358 and 359, the first at Sirmium, the latter at Rimini, came up with ambiguous formulae diverging from the Creed of Nicaea. Liberius, who had never lost favor with the Romans, recanted and was reinstated in 358, while Dionysius died in exile in Phrygia. Auxentius, in Milan, apparently unable to communicate with his flock in Latin, seems to have lacked broad popular support. Nonetheless, he remained in office long after the death of Constantius, backed by a faction comprising members of the court and urban clergy—the emperor, after all, was powerful—and presumably part of the congregation as well. Valentinian I, who succeeded Constantius after the interlude of Julian Apostata, followed a policy of strict noninterference in Church affairs—"I am but a layman"—and the civil service being concerned with law and order prudently kept out of the struggle at Milan as well as elsewhere. Hilary of Poitiers, who in 364 came to court to accuse Auxentius, was sent packing, and the condemnations pronounced by several synods against the "Arian" at Milan were ineffective.[7]

But Milan was an island in an otherwise pro-Nicene West, and with Auxentius's death in 374 the Nicene and possibly xenophobic Milanese opposition could mount a counterattack. During election meetings in the cathedral the factions clashed. The governor, the *consularis*, of Aemilia, Ambrose, tried to mediate and found himself acclaimed, whether or not spontaneously, as the congregation's choice for bishop—a compromise, based on the irreproachably pro-Nicene lineage of his family, on the hope of the anti-Nicenes for his neutrality, and on the emperor Valentinian's satisfaction in seeing in that place a level-headed, proven civil servant. Ambrose, then still a catechumen, was quickly baptized and a week later, on Sunday, December 8, 374, was consecrated bishop. Over the next twenty-four years he turned the See of Milan into the most influential in the West, far outshining Rome in political impact. His guiding policy was to free the ecclesiastical power from interference by the temporal, in particular to rescind the emperors' implied claim to stand at the head of the Church. In no uncertain terms he told Theodosius I that within the Church he was just one of the congregation.[8] The schism between East and West regarding the emperor's place in the Church starts right here. This guiding principle, as much as theological arguments, also underlies Ambrose's continued fight against "Arianism," which into the eighties remained strong at court in Milan. The young emperor Gratian, at first inclined to tolerate anti-Nicene views—witness a decree of 378 and the fight in 378–379 over a church, of which more later—was pulled back to the path of orthodoxy by Ambrose. But the anti-Nicene cause was taken up fervently by the empress dowager Justina and, presumably under her influence, by the boy emperor Valentinian II in 386 with a renewed decree of tolerance and a renewed fight for an "Arian" church in Milan.[9] In that last battle Ambrose won out over both heresy and temporal interference. Concomitantly, his major concern was the organization and the pastoral care of his flock and the strengthening of its faith: by sermons, by common prayer, by hymns sung in chorus by congregation and clergy, by the veneration of martyrs who had been victims of pagan and "Arian" persecution, and by the building of churches in their honor.

Milan, indeed, over the past forty years has yielded the remains of fourth-century church building, both through excavation and through the exploration of structures still extant, in such profusion as to make the city the foremost site in the West next to Rome for gaining a vivid impression of Early Christian architecture on a major scale (fig. 63).[10]

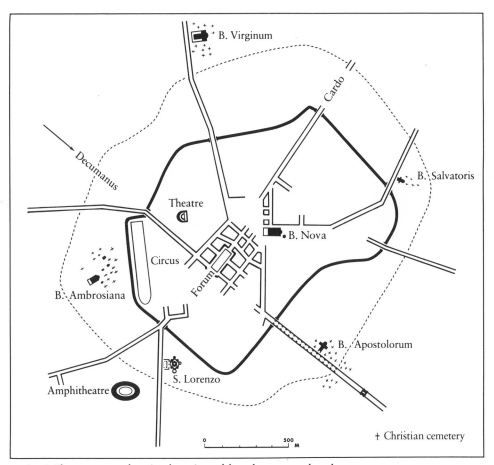

63. Milan ca. 400, showing location of fourth-century churches

Inside the city walls the cathedral, later dedicated to S. Tecla, and next to it the octagonal baptistery, were excavated in successive campaigns in 1943 and 1961–62, buried below the piazza just west of the Gothic Duomo. Some remains are accessible and visible from the subway station (fig. 64). Outside the walls rise, or rose: west of the city, the Basilica Ambrosiana, replaced by the grand Romanesque church of S. Ambrogio, but known from excavations undertaken nearly a century ago and from a few fragments incorporated in the structure of the present building; to the northeast on the highway to Como, the Basilica Virginum, S. Simpliciano, its original outer walls still standing to their full height of over twenty meters (fig. 65); to the southeast, outside the city gate leading to Rome, Porta Romana, the Basilica Apostolorum, or S. Nazaro, only masked by a twelfth-century remodeling (fig. 66); finally, just outside the gate leading to Pavia, on the Roman Via Ticinensis, S. Lorenzo, essentially still standing in all its fourth-century glory (see below, fig. 73).

Of the cathedral, inside the walls and in the very center of late antique Milan, large tracts of the foundations and, of the rising walls, the stump of a buttress against the apse have been unearthed—little, but enough to outline plan and building techniques: a nave and twin aisles to either side, all on colonnaded arcades; a chancel bay, raised and accessible over a *solea*, a pathway for the bishop's solemn entry, as in Constantine's

64. Milan, Piazza del Duomo, excavation of S. Tecla

65. Milan, S. Simpliciano, from the southwest

66. Milan, S. Nazaro, from the east

Lateran basilica; a semicircular apse, replaced in the late fourth or fifth century by another further east; communicating with the chancel area through arcaded colonnades, transept-like wings north and south, each perhaps subdivided by colonnades into twin aisles (fig. 67). The plan in the fourth century seems unique, but then fourth-century church planning was experimental throughout. In our context the size, building techniques, site, and date of S. Tecla are even more noteworthy than the plan. Extraordinarily large, 80 by 45 meters, it offered space, not counting chancel area and transept wings, for a congregation of close to three thousand—not many fewer than the Lateran cathedral, and that at Milan, hardly as populous as Constantinian Rome. The obvious irregularities of the plan—all angles deviating from ninety degrees, and nave and aisle colonnades not lining up with one another—may have been conditioned in part by the street system, poorly known in that zone, and by earlier buildings on the site.[11] At the same time, the building technique is remarkably sound: the entire structure is placed on deep foundations built of orderly coursed riverbed pebbles, set in tenacious mortar, while the rising walls are brickfaced in neat courses with low beds of strong white mortar (fig. 68). Apparently no expense was spared. Equally remarkable is the site chosen for the cathedral, a large terrain in the very center of urban Milan, presumably demanding the sacrifice of considerable property. Regarding the date of construction, documentary evidence is lacking, except that the synod of 355 was apparently convened in the cathedral and that in 386 the cathedral now excavated was still known as the new cathedral, as against the old, or small, cathedral, the *basilica*

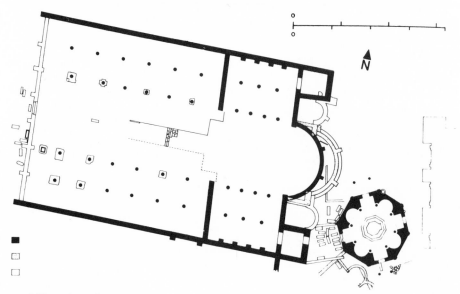

67. Milan, S. Tecla, plan

vetus or *minor*, then still extant and in use; its location has been sought but not yet found on the site of the Gothic Duomo, where the remains of a baptistery supposedly older than that belonging to the new cathedral have been identified.[12] Whatever the location of the *vetus*, the size of the synod of 355, attended by more than three hundred bishops, not counting their clerics, the emperor, his suite, and the congregation, suggests that it met in the large new cathedral. Hence, a date of construction prior to 355 is intimated. Concomitantly, its designation thirty years later as still the new cathedral suggests that it had been built within living memory; the more so, since the old cathedral could hardly have antedated the Edict of Milan, 313. A date around 350 thus seems reasonable for the new cathedral. Given its size, the presumable cost of the property required, and the expensive, careful construction of foundations and walls, financial backing must have been strong, possibly involving imperial assistance. As a conjecture, then, I submit that work was started between 345 and 350 under Constans, a strong partisan of Athanasius and the Nicene faction in the West, known for his generous support of the congregations,[13] and that it was completed, perhaps hastily, after 353 to be ready for the synod of 355. Whether the baptistery behind the cathedral was built by Saint Ambrose, as is generally assumed,[14] or whether he only composed the inscription for the building, which already existed, had best be left open.

Among the churches outside the city walls, S. Ambrogio, S. Nazaro, and S. Simpliciano form a closely knit group. All were founded by Saint Ambrose and thus were a generation later than the new cathedral; the first two are documented by his own letters and by contemporary witnesses as being completed in 386, while S. Simpliciano was apparently planned shortly before his death in 397. All were constructed in a technique different from that used in the cathedral: with pebble foundations, laid in a disorderly manner and intermingled with broken bricks and tiles, as witness S. Ambrogio (fig. 69); and with the facing of the rising walls frequently in reused bricks, with high mortarbeds and with patches or bands in herringbone pattern, *opus spicatum*, as at S. Nazaro and S. Simpliciano (fig. 70). These differences in technique have been taken to be indicative of the chronology of Milanese buildings in the fourth century. To be sure, local building techniques are apt to change in the type, size, and coursing of materials and in the thickness, composition, and tooling of the mortarbeds, and these changes greatly help in establishing a chronology of buildings in a given locale, as I, of all people, should be the last to deny. But the method, to be useful, must be adapted to the context of other determinants: local custom, financial means available, particular function, patronage, and limitation of time and resulting haste. As I see it, the lower-quality technique of Ambrose's churches

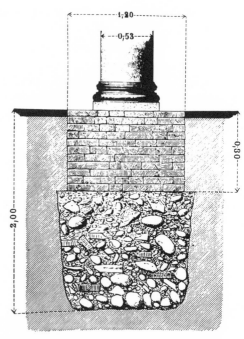

68. Milan, S. Tecla, foundation of nave column

69. Milan, S. Ambrogio, foundation of fourth-century nave column

70. Milan, S. Simpliciano, herringbone masonry

is probably determined not so much by a "development" of Milanese building methods as by less opulent financial backing and greater haste in construction. Ambrose was in a hurry, and the means at his disposal, while ample, were not unlimited.[15]

Nonetheless, his churches are impressive to this day as they rise, articulated by tall blind arches and lit by huge windows, to a height of twenty meters and more above the ground. All were installed as martyrs' and cemetery churches on older graveyards; all were provided with relics, whether those of local martyrs or brought from abroad; all were intended for the veneration of such relics and for burial of the faithful nearby; and all served for regular services and liturgical stations for congregations both from inside Milan and from the suburbs outside the gates of the expanding city. Indeed, all—except S. Ambrogio, the Basilica Ambrosiana—were easily accessible, being placed near the highways converging on the city from north, west, east, and south (fig. 63).[16] Ambrose wanted his see and the residence of the emperors to compete with the old capital of the world. Around Rome, Constantine had placed on the cemeteries along the highways sanctuaries commemorating the Roman martyrs—Saints Peter, Agnes, Lawrence, and the deacons Peter and Marcellinus—and in Ambrose's day the three ruling emperors were building the last of them, S. Paolo fuori le Mura over the grave of the apostle on the Ostian Way (fig. 26). Likewise, Ambrose wanted Milan to be ringed by the sanctuaries of Milanese martyrs or, given the scarcity of the latter, by martyrs' relics brought from elsewhere.

Like the overall location of Ambrose's churches, their plans, different as they are from one another, reveal political connotations. S. Ambrogio, probably planned as early as 379 as the first among them and known from excavations, was an ordinary basilica, as just at that time became standard in the West: nave, two aisles, semicircular apse, and colonnaded arcades. The altar in front of the apse originally was to shelter only the founder's sarcophagus. The arrangement apparently was unusual in Milan, and Ambrose found justification necessary: the bishop, having officiated at the altar, was entitled, so he claims, to burial underneath. Popular insistence or protest before the dedication of the church induced him to share the place under the altar with two local martyrs conveniently found nearby.[17] However, is it not permissible to interpret Ambrose's original claim to that place of honor as an implicit riposte to Constantine's first burial place under or near the altar in the chancel area of the church of the Holy Apostles in Constantinople? Scandalous for a layman and therefore changed by Constantine's son himself, the distinction of that burial place was appropriate for a priest, a concept fully consonant with Ambrose's policy of keeping, within the Church, the emperor in his place among the laity.

In the Basilica Apostolorum in Milan, now S. Nazaro, the political connotations and the allusions to Constantine's Apostle church in Constantinople are obvious. Ambrose's church, thinly disguised by a Romanesque remodeling, essentially still survives and is easily envisaged (fig. 71).[18] It was laid out on a cross plan, the nave arm longer and accessible by three doors in the façade, the side wings lower without entrances at their ends, but opening in triple arcades toward the center bay. There the altar sheltered apostle relics in the famous silver casket, whose place of origin—long in doubt—appears to have been Constantinople. The chancel arm—I side with Enrico Villa and Mario Mirabella Roberti—originally was terminated by a straight wall, the apse being added only around 395 when the relics of the local martyr Nazarius were deposited there under a second altar.[19] Clearly the model to which Ambrose looked was Constantine's Apostoleion. The cross plan, if not identical, can only be a variant on that of the Constantinopolitan church, as it presented itself in the eighties when the emperor's sarcophagus had long been removed from the chancel in the center bay and deposited in the mausoleum rotunda, built by Constantius against the entrance arm of the church built by his father.[20] Differences in plan between the Milanese "copy" and the model—arms single naved or divided into nave and aisles, with the nave arm longer or the same length as the others—would matter but little in the context of late antique (and medieval) thinking. What counted was the cross shape and a few selected elements.[21] More than anything else, it was the symbolism of the cross plan that mattered and that was stressed by Ambrose in his dedicatory poem as Christ's sign of victory, just as Gregory of Nazianz at the same time stressed the cross shape of the Constantinopolitan Apostle church.[22] The original relics, deposited on May 9, 386, under the high altar in the center bay, were of the apostles Andrew and Thomas and of John the Evangelist. Constantine's Apostoleion, too, by that time had long housed relics of the evangelist Luke and of the apostles Andrew and Timothy, brought from Ephesus and Greece in 356 and 357, respectively. Moreover, in Milan, under the date of November 27, Luke, Andrew, John, and Euphemia of Chalkedon are listed; and since Aquileia, likewise, in the eighties of the fourth century received relics of the same saints, a donation of relics from Constantinople to the North Italian sees, possibly made by Theodosius, is likely.[23] In any event, the parallel between the Apostle churches in Milan and Constantinople is striking in plan, dedication, and relics. For Ambrose in his fight against the anti-Nicenes at court in Milan during the eighties, stressing the bonds to Constantinople, cleansed just then of "Arianism" by Theodosius, was as essential as stressing those to Rome, implied in the siting of his churches around Milan.

The link to Constantinople seems to have lost importance for the Milanese Church by the nineties when, shortly before Ambrose's death on Easter 397, the Basilica Virginum, S. Simpliciano, was planned—construction may have started only later. While still powerful in design and cross shaped in plan, it no longer resembles Ambrose's or, for that matter, Constantine's Apostle church in either function or layout. The proportions have changed; the chancel arm has shrunk to a shallow forechoir, preceding the apse and housing the altar; and the wings have been turned into the arms of a transept slightly lower than and wide open towards the nave (figs. 65 and 72). Concomitantly, the martyrs' relics, no longer of apostles or evangelists, but of some minor recent martyrs from the Trentino and obtained by Simplicianus, Ambrose's successor on the episcopal see, were placed in a small martyrs' chapel outside, accessible from the left transept arm, rather than occupying the center of the church and thus being its very focus.[24] In that abbreviated form, deprived of its original traits in plan and function, the type becomes the fountainhead of a large family of churches spread over North Italy and the Alpine regions. At S. Simpliciano itself only the location of the church, on the highway to Como, remains within Ambrose's program, a program aimed in the eighties, if I am right, at linking Milan to both the old and the new capitals of the world, Rome and Constantinople, making it a bridge between West and East.

Among the suburban churches of Milan, S. Lorenzo is the only one not founded by Saint Ambrose (fig. 73).[25] The evidence regarding its date was summed up and its possible function discussed by Dale Kinney a few years ago. Neither Ambrose in his letters and sermons nor any contemporary mentions the church as having been founded or built by him.

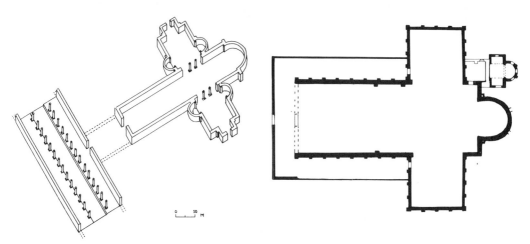

71. Milan, S. Nazaro (Basilica Apostolorum), isometric reconstruction

72. Milan, S. Simpliciano, plan

73. Milan, S. Lorenzo, exterior from the southeast

Under its present name, it first appears around 590, although the dedication to Saint Lawrence seems to be alluded to when around 500 Bishop Lawrence I of Milan built against the north flank the chapel of S. Sisto—Pope Sixtus II being Saint Lawrence's fellow martyr. Likewise of late date are the dedications of the east chapel to Hippolytus, another martyr close to Saint Lawrence, and of the south chapel to Aquilino, a local saint who seems to have lived around A.D. 1000. As unknown as the previous dedications are the original functions of the structures. The main church was certainly not built or used as a martyr's church. A small graveyard, found nearby, was pagan, and no relic of any kind was, to our knowledge, connected in early times either with S. Lorenzo or with the two chapels, those of S. Aquilino and S. Ippolito, appended from the outset to the main church (fig. 74).[26]

S. Lorenzo, as we must call it for want of another name, must be seen, in fact, not as a church with appended chapels, but as a group of buildings linked to one another from the outset. The main church, S. Aquilino, and S. Ippolito were all erected in one single campaign. All rest on a huge common platform composed of stone blocks; of fragments of friezes, archivolts, and half columns; of capitals and brackets to fasten awn-

ings—all spoils, presumably, from the demolition of the nearby amphitheater.[27] From this solid platform, well preserved and still accessible
below S. Aquilino (fig. 75), rise the church and the chapels. To me the
church is still the most beautiful in Milan and among the most beautiful
in the Western world. It was laid out as a huge tetraconch double-shell
structure. Four wide, half-domed exedrae billow from a center bay, originally square; and this core is enveloped by the outer shell of an ambulatory and galleries (fig. 76). Both communicated with the core through
arcaded colonnades, their columns, certainly on the ground floor, resting
originally, it appears, on tall pedestals. The groinvaults in the ambulatory
are of twelfth-century date, but they may well have taken the place of
Early Christian vaults, perhaps in hollow tube construction; whether or
not the galleries were vaulted remains open. Certainly, the huge center
bay was covered either by a pendentive dome or by a groinvault: the
four corner towers, aside from giving access to and connecting the four
sections of the gallery, abutted the corners of that main vault.[28] Two
thorough rebuildings, one after a devastating fire in 1071, perhaps followed by further medieval repairs, the other carried out between 1577
and 1595, have altered the interior by throwing strengthening arches
diagonally across the corners of the center bay, thus turning it into
an octagon (fig. 77). They have also changed the outside silhouette by
raising over that bay a tall drum containing the dome. This sixteenth-
century remodeling largely determines today's impression: the steep
drum, higher than the corner towers, and the heavy grey piers and arches
of the exedrae and their diagonal links. But plan and structure of the
Early Christian building remain unimpaired and are easily envisaged.
Solidly built, the corner piers of heavy stone blocks, the walls brickfaced
in carefully laid courses, the mortarbeds thin and white in color, all of
superb workmanship, the church nonetheless was much airier than today: filled with light from large windows in the ambulatory, in the galleries, and presumably in a square drum over the center; the arcades in
the exedrae with lighter supports and thus wider (fig. 78). The walls
were sheathed in *opus sectile*—dowels survive—and the center vault
carried a mosaic, "intus alavariis [aula variis?] lapidibus auroque tecta
edita in turribus," possibly of gold foil, until destroyed by the fire of
1071.[29] Outside, the grouping of the four towers at the corners of the
square drum—a fifth tower in medieval terminology—created a silhouette truly *edita in turribus*. Lower than today's, it was nonetheless
equally lively and exciting and was more compact (fig. 79). The approach from Via Romana was and is to this day marked by the monumental colonnade of a propylaeum, its center bay rising in an arch (fig. 80).
Behind it, a huge atrium extended, enveloped by porticoes and slightly

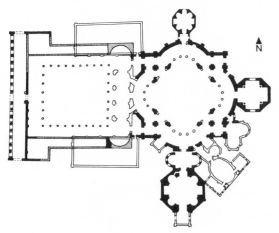

75. Milan, S. Lorenzo, stone platform below S. Aquilino

74. Milan, S. Lorenzo, plan

76. Milan, S. Lorenzo, interior

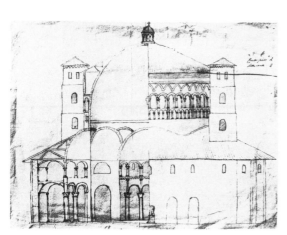

77. Milan, S. Lorenzo, interior as of 1577–95

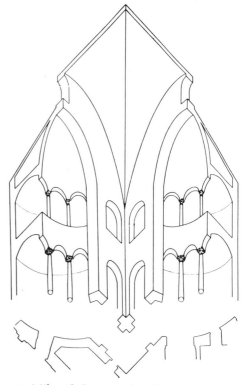

78. Milan, S. Lorenzo, interior, reconstruction

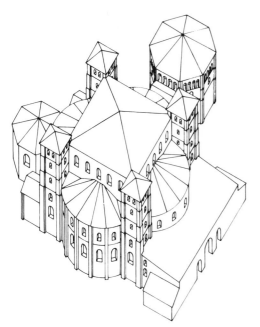

79. Milan, S. Lorenzo, exterior, reconstruction

80. Milan, S. Lorenzo, propylaeum, colonnade

longer than it was wide. From there, kept at short distance, the visitor saw, rising over the roof of the double-tiered narthex, the articulated five-tower group of the church.[30]

S. Lorenzo, then, belongs to a group of churches laid out in a double-shell system with either a tetraconch or an octaconch core, best known from a building such as H. Sergius and Bakchos in Constantinople in the early years of Justinian. This is not the place to go into the origins and the spread of the genus. It need only be said that in church planning it appears first in Constantine's Golden Octagon at Antioch, which, rising next to the imperial palace, served both as the cathedral of the bishop and for the emperor's attendance at services. Whether the propylaeum at Milan, with its arcuated lintel, is an honorific feature marking imperial buildings, as once suggested by Dyggve, had best be left open. But one might recall that just such a propylaeum and atrium led to the fifth-century H. Sophia in Constantinople, the predecessor of Justinian's church; whether or not Constantine's, the earliest church on the site, was already marked by that feature remains a moot question.[31]

S. Aquilino and S. Ippolito both from the outset were integral parts of the S. Lorenzo complex: the stone platform is continuous; the brickwork of the rising walls in the three buildings shows but minor differences; and a wide opening was left in the flattened south flank of the main church to be closed during construction by the adjoining wall of S. Aquilino. The latter, as witness a shift in the stone platform, seems to have first been planned without the connecting narthex which in the end was decided on: square, groinvaulted, apsed on either side; the walls covered with mosaics showing, albeit in fragments, figures of apostles and patriarchs and biblical scenes so far unexplained. The chapel proper is laid out as a steep octagon. Above a ground-floor zone of tall niches, alternately rectangular and semicircular, a corridor in the thickness of the wall opens both inward and in large outward windows (figs. 81 and 82). A cloister vault, built in solid brick, covers the main space, while the outside walls are topped by a dwarf gallery level with the springing of the vault. The interior, somewhat heavy nowadays, was lightened by colorful marble sheathing, by mosaics in the niche vaults and the dome, and by painted imitation revetment in the clerestory corridor.[32] Remains of the latter two survive, as well as *sinopie* of paintings tried out in that corridor (fig. 83). Notwithstanding the Christian character of the mosaics and the *sinopie*, then, S. Aquilino in plan, decoration, and even size calls to mind the mausoleum built by Maximian outside the walls of Milan around A.D. 300 (fig. 62). And indeed, as shown by Dale Kinney and others, S. Aquilino was not a baptistery, but a mausoleum, presumably an imperial one.

Dale Kinney likewise has argued convincingly in favor of a date for the

81. Milan, S. Aquilino, interior

83. Milan, S. Aquilino, interior, brick masonry, and fourth-century *sinopia* of Victory (Christ?)

82. Milan, S. Aquilino, exterior

S. Lorenzo complex prior to the 380s. If I incline towards a dating more precise and diverging from hers, the chronological difference is but small. As she has shown, the amphitheater whose stones were used to build the platform of the S. Lorenzo group in all probability had already been demolished when in the mid-eighties Ausonius composed his verse description of Milan, which lists the extant buildings, but not the amphitheater. Hunting games, when resumed, as is documented, in 399 and 400, could have taken place in a temporary wooden structure, whether on the old site or elsewhere. The technique of masonry in the S. Lorenzo buildings lacks the hallmarks of the churches built by Ambrose, in particular the bands of herringbone construction. Throughout, the brickwork is of far superior workmanship (fig. 83). However, this does not necessarily place S. Lorenzo close in date to the cathedral. Rather, it seems to reflect, as suggested also by S. Lewis, the rich financial backing which made possible such expensive construction and the sumptuous interior decoration in both the main church and S. Aquilino. Ambrose, witness the poor construction technique and the apparent lack of precious decoration in his church buildings, could not, it seems, as a rule afford such luxury. On the other hand, imperial backing appears likely for S. Lorenzo: in view of the costliness and size of the buildings; of the strong likelihood of S. Aquilino's having been designed as an imperial mausoleum, like its obvious model, Maximian's, at S. Vittore al Corpo; and of the fact that only by the emperor's orders could the amphitheater, fiscal property that it was, be demolished and its material reused for building the S. Lorenzo group.[33]

Imperial backing on that scale could have been forthcoming at any time between 340 and 402, while Milan was an imperial residence—that is, before, during, and after the pontificate of Ambrose. All the same, Ausonius's testimony, though *ex silentio*, seems to speak for the eighties of the fourth century as the *terminus ante quem* for the construction of S. Lorenzo. Concomitantly, among the emperors resident in Milan who might have built for themselves the mausoleum of S. Aquilino, Theodosius and Honorius can be eliminated. Both had provided for their burials elsewhere, in Constantinople and Rome, respectively.[34] Hence, the late eighties, when Theodosius moved to Milan, seem to be corroborated as our *terminus ante*.

Ambrose, one recalls, did not build S. Lorenzo. But he seems to have mentioned it by its original name, the Basilica Portiana. That church, indeed, played a key role in the conflict which in Easter week 386 pitted Ambrose against young Valentinian II and the empress dowager Justina, champion of the anti-Nicene faction in Milan. "Now the Arians," so the bishop reports, "no longer claim [just] the Portiana which is outside the walls, but the Basilica Nova, the cathedral, which is inside." Ambrose

declines to cede either church and the "Arians" give in about the cathedral, but stubbornly claim the Portiana. "Et ego," says the little emperor,
"debeo habere unam basilicam"—"I, too, must have a church." "Non
illam"—"not that one"—cruelly answers Ambrose. The details of the
ensuing contest do not pertain to our discussion: the palace having the
emperor's pew prepared in the Portiana; the Nicene faction countering
this move by occupying the church; the military being dispatched to
surround the Portiana as well as both the old and new cathedrals; Ambrose's provocatory sermons and steadfast resistance; and the emperor's
final surrender.[35] Relevant, on the other hand, is the insistence of the
emperor and the anti-Nicenes on having the Portiana for their use and
the location of that church outside town, a fact stressed by Ambrose
almost as excusing, if not ceding to, the anti-Nicene claims.

The claims of the "Arians" to the Portiana, in fact, sound as if they
were neither new nor unjustified. As early as 378, as reported by Ambrose, a basilica, apparently contended by anti-Nicenes and Nicenes, had
been sequestered by the emperor Gratian, either on the anti-Nicenes'
behalf or so as to remove it during arbitration from the grasp of either
faction. The year after, under heavy, if indirect, pressure from Ambrose,
he ceded it to the Nicenes. Whether or not it was the Portiana, as is
likely, the church existed, either in "Arian" or in Nicene hands, when,
prior to August 383, Ambrose agreed to have there a disputation on the
question of the Trinity, challenged by two "Arian" chamberlains of the
emperor Gratian, who died that month.[36] In any event, the "Arians'"
claim to the Portiana was taken up in 385 by Valentinian II, presumably
goaded by his mother Justina. Ambrose was called before the emperor
and the assembled *consistorium* and ordered to hand over the church.
He refused, backed by an unruly and, one suspects, well-orchestrated
crowd. However, the attack continued, and an imperial decree in January 386 granted freedom of worship also to anti-Nicenes, possibly based
on the decree issued in 378 and revoked the year after. Apparently the
"Arians" had a justified claim of some years' standing to the Portiana which interlocked with claims by the imperial court. Relying on
their increased strength in that ambient, they renewed their demands in
385–86.[37]

Given the insistence of both anti-Nicenes and Nicenes and the obvious
involvement of emperor and court, the Portiana cannot have been an
insignificant church. It must have been outstanding among Milanese
churches by the role it played in the ecclesiastical life of the city and, one
conjectures, by its beauty and size. Nor is it likely that such a church
would disappear, as the Portiana does, without leaving a trace, archaeological or documentary. It must have lived on under a different name.
Concomitantly, outside the walls of antique Milan no Early Christian

church survives—not counting Ambrose's—except S.   Lorenzo. Thus, as has frequently been suggested, I think it more than likely that S. Lorenzo is in fact the Portiana, fought over by Ambrose and the emperors in the years between 378 and 386.

This raises the interlocking questions of the date of construction and the original function of S. Lorenzo. The consensus of opinion among defenders of a fourth-century date, including myself, has been so far to assign the construction of the S. Lorenzo group to the episcopate of the "Arian" Auxentius I, 355–74. As to its function, the opinion once held of its having been the "Arian" cathedral of Auxentius cannot be maintained. Being the only legitimate bishop, he naturally officiated in the cathedral, S. Tecla. Hence S. Lorenzo could be only interpreted as being a "palace" church, designed for worship by the court and in any event close to the palace. However, would not the "Arians" at court have worshipped at the cathedral as long as that church was in "Arian" hands? Of course, they might have preferred a church of their own comparatively close to the palace, the more so since in the cathedral clashes between Nicene and anti-Nicene partisans were not to be excluded.[38]

But let me propose an alternative. There was, after all, a time when the "Arian" faction was in need of a church of its own. That time would fall after Ambrose's consecration as bishop in December 374. With this event, the cathedral became pro-Nicene territory, and the pro-Nicene faction under his leadership grew increasingly aggressive. The emperor Gratian, in accordance with his late father's prudent policy of noninterference in matters of dogma, was trying to steer a course between the factions. Also, his strictly orthodox upbringing may have weakened under the influence of his wife, Flavia Maxima Constantia, posthumous daughter of Constantius II, who was brought up an anti-Nicene. Thus, in the late summer of 378, after the catastrophic defeat of Valens at Adrianople at the hands of the Goths and under the influence of both his wife and his stepmother Justina, Gratian issued his decree of tolerance towards the "heretics"—perhaps an attempt to promote national unity. Is it not permissible, then, to conjecture that in conformity with his policy of neutrality reinforced by domestic pressure, young Gratian—not a strong character anyhow—might have faltered in his orthodoxy and allowed S. Lorenzo to be built as a cathedral for the "Arians" and their bishop *in pectore*? The time would have been between 375 and 378 or possibly in 378. Wavering between Nicenes and anti-Nicenes—the dispute on the Trinity was surely beyond his understanding—he did not see why the "Arians" should not have a cathedral of their own.[39] A *terminus post quem* for the planning of S. Lorenzo seems to be provided by the imperial mausoleum attached, S. Aquilino, laid out and built from the start in conjunction with the main church: the mausoleum obviously was not yet planned when late in 375 or early in 376 the body of Valentinian was brought to Constantinople to be buried in the mausoleum attached to the Holy Apostles by Constantius II for the burial of Constantine I and all his successors. Hence S. Aquilino would have been planned not before 376 and not after 378, provided, as I believe, S. Lorenzo is the church contended over and sequestered that year. It would have been built under Gratian, with S. Aquilino presumably intended as the mausoleum of the Western dynasty. Neither Gratian nor his half-brother Valentinian II found their resting place there, and the body of Gratian's first wife, Flavia Maxima Constantia, was shipped to Constantinople in 383—to rest near her father Constantius II in the mausoleum at the Apostle church. But it is possible that Justina, the empress dowager, reconciled to Ambrose and presumably to orthodoxy after 387, appropriated for herself S. Aquilino, the "Cappella Reginae." [40]

If S. Lorenzo, as I believe, was built as the cathedral of the anti-Nicene faction, strong at the court, its location, too, becomes understandable. It lies close to the presumable site of the palace near the circus. But it lies outside the city walls. Such location in the suburbs was apparently fourth-century practice for dissident religious minority groups. In Rome, the Nicene Liberius had his see at S. Agnese, while from 355 to 358 the anti-Nicenes held the city and the regular residence of the bishop at the Lateran; when they were ousted, their bishop, Felix, took his seat on the Via Portuensis. Similarly, at Constantinople in 379, Bishop Demophilos, who deviated from strict Nicene orthodoxy, was forced by Theodosius "to hold [his] assemblies without the city." [41] If Gratian or his advisers at Milan held any hopes of placating the Nicene faction by moving the "Arians" beyond the walls and far from the cathedral, S. Tecla, left undisputedly to the orthodox, or of evading Ambrose's wrath, little did they know him. The tolerance decree issued by Gratian from Sirmium in August or September 378 was the last straw. Ambrose counterattacked. Gratian, presumably alarmed by reports of the great bishop's outraged indignation over such lax imperial policies and badly shaken by the catastrophe of Adrianople, asked for instruction from his headquarters at Sirmium. Ambrose forthwith addressed to his young sovereign the first two books of *De fide*, staunchly upholding the pure Nicene definition of the Trinity, followed up the coming year by composing the last three books, and, in response to a penitent letter of Gratian's, continued the year after with *De spiritu sancto*. [42] In this climate, I submit, the building and possession of S. Lorenzo, the Portiana, became the object of contention which it was to remain for nearly a decade. Construction was started, let me conjecture, in 376 or 377; it had hardly been completed or was still underway when late in 378 Ambrose's forceful opposition, joined to his congregation's presumably vociferous protests, forced Gratian to sequester the church, thus withholding it from both contending parties. The next year he gave in to Ambrose and ceded it to the Nicenes.

The anti-Nicenes naturally would have been incensed over that imperial about-face and would have continued to press their claim to the church originally planned for them. The ascension to the throne in 382 of the boy emperor Valentinian II, backed by Justina, provided a new chance for them to demand equality of worship in their own cathedral and for the imperial house to make up for the defeat suffered in 379. Towards the end of 384, an "Arian" bishop, Mercurinus, driven by Theodosius from his see in Rumania, was called by the court to Milan and installed as Auxentius II, the anti-Nicene bishop, early in 386, presumably against considerable opposition—therefore the time lag of over a year between his arrival and his consecration.[43] This is the climate in which to view the events of 385 and 386. The "Arian" bishop needed a cathedral, as did his court; the Portiana, S. Lorenzo, originally had been intended for just that purpose. The appointment of the new "Arian" bishop would have exacerbated the conflict, and the existence of the imperial mausoleum attached to the church was an added, if not the principal, reason for Justina's and her son's insistent claim to just that church. Hence, Ambrose's being ordered already in 385 to hand it over; hence, the decree of tolerance issued—better, reissued—in January 386; hence, the contest of wills during Easter week that year, when the anti-Nicenes wanted a place of worship and baptism of their own; hence, the young emperor's pitiful complaint, "I, too, must have a basilica"; hence, Ambrose's triumph after the final victory of his uncompromising policy of ruthlessly combating both "Arianism" and interference by the temporal power in the Church.

This leaves a word to be said about the chapel, later S. Ippolito, attached to the eastward exedra of S. Lorenzo. The plan, cross shaped inside and vaulted throughout, points to its, too, having been a mausoleum. Nearly forty years ago, it was correctly pointed out that the bishops of Milan, from the middle of the fifth century on, sought burial at S. Lorenzo. Could they have taken up a much earlier custom started in the fourth century by their "heretic" predecessors? And could the chapel of S. Ippolito, when planned between 375–76 and 378, have been intended for the belated burial of bishop Auxentius I?[44] Or is this too bold a conjecture?

Be that as it may, this, I submit, is the political frame within which the building of the S. Lorenzo group outside the walls and the "battle of the cathedrals" in Milan should be seen.

IV

ROME AGAIN

Once Constantinople had been founded, no emperor returned to Rome to take up permanent residence. Nonetheless, the illusion of her being the legitimate capital of the Empire—though no longer the only one—had been carefully nurtured by Constantine. Long after him, moreover, by general consensus Rome remained *caput mundi*, as conceived by Augustus and Virgil. That concept lived on, in the face of catastrophes, political and economic, through the centuries. However, as her importance in the realm of secular politics dwindled, a new reality came to the fore. Rome again became a capital: the capital of the bishop of Rome, soon the spiritual leader of the West, and in a sense very different from Virgil's she returned to being *caput mundi*.

One looks back at the map of Rome under Constantine and the remote location at the Lateran of her bishop's residence and his cathedral, far out in the southeastern corner of the city and near the walls (fig. 1). The site had been chosen by Constantine from considerations of expedience in the political and religious context of Rome in 312–13. By the end of the fourth and increasingly in the fifth century the short-range advantage turned into a long-range liability. The monumental and administrative area in the center of the city was rapidly losing its political and sacral connotations. To be sure, the Senate still met in the Curia; the city prefect still received in his audience hall on the Forum Romanum, now the church of SS. Cosma e Damiano, preceded by a circular domed entrance hall, added in the early fourth century; and near the Forum Boarium the prefect of the annona still occupied the colonnaded hall presumably built under Constantine and later incorporated into the front part of S. Maria in Cosmedin.[1] And altogether the conservative party, still dominant in the Senate through the better part of the fourth century, fought a desperate battle to retain the traditional, and by implication pagan, character of this the heart of Rome. Alföldi's *Conflict of Ideas*, the essays assembled by Momigliano in the Oxford-Warburg Studies, and Peter Brown's *Augustine of Hippo* all outline the situation. In the realm of public building, the conflict comes to the fore in a conscious continued policy on the part of the traditionalists aimed at restoring the inherited character, both secular and religious, of the Forum and at preserving or reviving as best possible the architectural concepts handed down through the centuries: the Secretarium Senatus was restored; so was the Basilica Julia in 377 along the lines and in the vocabulary laid down nearly four hundred years before. The Temple of Saturn was rebuilt on the old podium, its columns surmounted by Ionic capitals, albeit deviating from the classical norm, but resuscitating an order rarely used in Rome through Imperial times; they carry an entablature of second-century date, splendidly carved and saved from some older building (fig. 84). Not far away, below the eastward cliff of the Capitoline Hill, the *porticus deorum consentium* was built from the ground in 367, entirely composed of such spoils (fig. 85). But the fight for the old gods was in vain. Christianity had become the state religion. Paganism in 395 was declared illegal. The great families were forced to convert, and the few elderly aristocrats who openly or clandestinely clung to their religious heritage played no public role. The temples in the course of the fourth century were closed and deprived of their funds, and by 400 Capitol and Fora were no longer even a shadow of the religious center they had been at the start of the fourth century. Nor did what had been the heart of Rome and the Empire retain by that time any major political importance. The palaces on the Palatine were maintained, but no emperor, no court, no imperial officer of standing resided there. And the Senate, after the blow of 395, could no longer cling to the illusion of political power it had still nurtured some ten years earlier when fighting under Symmachus's leadership for the altar of Victory in the Curia.[2]

Rome by the early fifth century was a Christian city, as any visitor could see. Clearly, many of the unobtrusive community centers of old, installed in mansions or tenements, continued to function, some until the ninth century; others, indeed, were newly acquired in the fourth century. But nearly half such *domus ecclesiae* between 380 and 440 were being replaced and their number supplemented by large basilicas, splendidly appointed and increasingly claiming public standing. A few large but modest halls, to be sure, already served Christian congregations by the middle of the fourth century: of one, large parts lie buried next to the

84. Rome, Forum, Temple of Saturn

85. Rome, Forum, *porticus deorum consentium*

twelfth-century church of S. Crisogono; of another, founded in 336 by
Pope Mark at the foot of the Capitoline Hill, some elements, including a
sumptuous pavement, survive below the present church of S. Marco; of
the first church of S. Maria in Trastevere, built between 337 and 352
by Pope Julius I and buried below the huge extant twelfth-century basilica, little is known so far save its existence. But the majority of the new
churches date from the last third of the fourth through the first third
of the fifth century: S. Anastasia, S. Clemente, S. Lorenzo in Damaso,
S. Sisto Vecchio, S. Pietro in Vincoli, SS. Giovanni e Paolo, S. Vitale,
S. Sabina, S. Lorenzo in Lucina, and S. Marcello al Corso.[3] Built in
roughly that sequence, the new churches were remarkably homogeneous.
Constructed in mortared rubble with double brick facing, as long customary in Rome, all follow a standard plan composed of a nave, ter-
minating apse, high clerestory carried by colonnaded arcades, and two
aisles. Where a building of the type, such as a thermae basilica, was
available it was purchased and refurbished as the audience hall of Christ,
as witness S. Pudenziana with its grand apse mosaic (fig. 22). All are
meant to hold large congregations ranging in size from eight to nearly
fourteen hundred. Deviations from the standard are comparatively minor,
and even the dimensions vary little. But the differences in the quality of
design, the proportions, and the splendor of decorations are considerable. Taste and financial backing apparently varied. The contrast between S. Clemente or S. Vitale (fig. 86) on the one hand and S. Sabina
on the other (fig. 87) speaks for itself. The former buildings, low and
bare from what is known, with crude columns and plain capitals; the
latter beautifully proportioned, carried by a splendid set of columns—
spoils from some Roman building—profusely lit by large windows,
planned with a coffered ceiling, and lavishly decorated with marble pan-
eling above the arcades (fig. 88), painted decoration in the aisles, and
mosaics in the apse, on the nave walls, and below a quintuple window
on the façade, the latter with the dedicatory inscription still surviving.
Outside, nave and apse rise, and always rose, high over the surrounding
gardens and mansions (fig. 89).

   All these new churches, whether modest or grand and richly appointed,
seem to reflect a conscious building policy on the part of the papacy. The
bishop of Rome as head of the Church increasingly had his name linked
to the new basilicas, whether or not he was the actual founder. It has
indeed been suggested that an unwritten understanding obliged a newly
elected pope to build a church or to found a community center, just as
such an obligation bound a Roman magistrate to finance public building
or circus games. In fact, during the fourth century nearly every pope
gave his name to a new foundation: Sylvester I to the *titulus Sylvestri*;
Mark I to S. Marco; Julius I to the *basilica Julii* (or *titulus Callisti*) on

86. Rome, S. Vitale, reconstruction

87. Rome, S. Sabina, interior

88. Rome, S. Sabina, interior, *opus sectile* decoration above arcades

89. Rome, S. Sabina, exterior

the site of S. Maria in Trastevere; Damasus to the *titulus Damasi*, installed in his family mansion near S. Lorenzo in Damaso. Still, S. Sisto Vecchio at the end of the century was apparently built by Pope Anastasius I using his own resources. Where a pope's means were insufficient, a wealthy parishioner or clergyman would provide the funds. But the name of the ruling pope would be prominently connected with the foundation. This seems to have been true already when under Pope Sylvester the *titulus Equitii* was founded, and it became general practice from the last years of the fourth through the first third of the fifth century, the only exception being S. Paolo fuori le Mura, the last great donation of the emperors in Rome. A bequest from a moderately wealthy lady, Vestina, financed the construction of S. Vitale, but the biography of Pope Innocent in the *Liber Pontificalis* stresses that he organized the work and dedicated the church. Similarly, at S. Sabina construction and decoration were financed by a wealthy presbyter from Illyricum, Peter, but the dedicatory inscription begins, not with his name, but with the name of the ruling pope Caelestin, while the *Liber Pontificalis* goes further by placing the construction in the biography of Sixtus III, under whom, perhaps, the finishing touches were put on the decoration. Again, at SS. Giovanni e Paolo, where construction was financed by the enormously wealthy senator Pammachius, whether during his life or after 410 through a bequest, the dedication poem for the decoration of the vestibule starts out with the name of the pope, whether or not Leo I, and mentions the actual founder only at the end. From 390 to 410, under Popes Siricius and Innocent, the procedure would seem to have been institutionalized by setting up a standing committee in charge of financing and supervising the building activity of the Church in the city and at the great martyrs' shrines: at S. Pudenziana, S. Vitale, S. Agnese, and S. Lorenzo fuori le Mura. The committee was composed of apparently wealthy clergymen headed by the presbyter Leopardus, though changing in membership; but the ruling pope, in his biography in the *Liber Pontificalis*, is presented as the *spiritus movens*. Beginning with Sixtus III (432–40), the situation changes further, and the pope claims outright for himself the honor of being the founder: at S. Pietro in Vincoli, where the actual founder Philippus and even the imperial subsidies provided are barely mentioned; at S. Lorenzo in Lucina; at S. Maria Maggiore; and at the Lateran baptistery—but the last two, as we shall see, are special cases. From here on *hic fecit*, or *hic reparavit*, *hic dedicavit*, become standard phrases in the papal biographies from Leo to Symmachus at the end of the century; only for imperial donations, rare in the fifth century, does the papacy abandon its claim of being the founder. Even the occasional reference in inscriptions to the cleric supervising construction disappears after Leo I. Indirectly and directly, then, through the fifth century the papal see appears to have financed and certainly supervised a program of monumental church building in Rome, emphatically stressing its claim to that effect.[4]

A program on such a scale, when distributed over sixty-odd years, was well within the means of the Church. By the late fourth century a large patrimony had accumulated in the hands of the Roman bishop. Constantine's gift of estates and income for the maintenance of his church foundations in Rome had been considerable; the market value has been estimated as roughly 300,000 gold solidi, the income at 25,000 solidi, "at a time when three or four gold solidi bought a man's food for the year." These gifts had been enlarged by donations from other sources, encouraged by governmental and ecclesiastical legislation: voluntary offerings and bequests by the faithful from the very rich to those of modest means, reversion to the Church of the property of bishops and other clergy in case of childless or intestate death, tax privileges and exemption from onerous civic duties, the prohibition of church consecration without previous provision of endowment.[5] This capital invested in real estate seems to have increased further during the fifth century, notwithstanding the loss of the North African possessions through the Vandal invasion and the successive raids into Italy as far as Rome by Visigoths, Huns, and Vandals. On the contrary, rich families driven away by general insecurity or unable to keep up maintenance or individuals withdrawing into religious life, like the Roman ladies from Jerome's circle, would leave their estates to the Church, or else the Church would be able to acquire them by purchase. The huge landholdings thus accruing around Rome and through Central Italy produced a sizable income, and a budgeting system going back to the third century and solidly established in Rome by the end of the fifth assigned one-fourth of the income to the upkeep, lighting, and, obviously, building of churches, the other three-fourths going one each to charity, maintenance of the clergy, and the household of the bishop.[6]

Intensifying pastoral care and facilitating the work of overall administration were no doubt guiding elements in this building program. In fact, the new churches appear to have been distributed very deliberately in conformity with the administrative regions of Rome as established by Augustus and continued on the civic level for centuries (fig. 90).[7] By 440 all the *regiones* each boasted, along with the surviving community centers and the few churches of fourth-century date, at least one of the new basilicas, all, that is, except the regions comprising the center of the monumental show area—the Fora, the Capitoline Hill, the Palatine— regions IV and VIII. That sector was overcrowded, and the Church, one suspects, still may have shied away from the old civic and pagan religious center, long after paganism had been declared dead. But the other

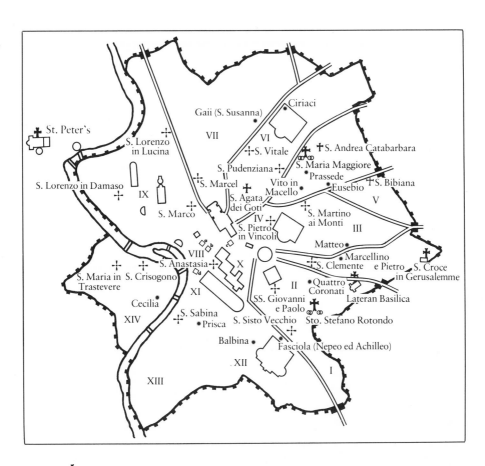

Constantinian churches

Major non-titular churches

✝ Minor non-titular churches

⫶ Tituli replaced by churches

＊ Tituli continuing

◇ Secular and pagan buildings built or
rebuilt after Constantine:
a *Porticus Deorum Consentium*
b *Temple of Saturn*
c *Praefectura Urbis*
   (SS. Cosma e Damiano)
d *Statio Annonae*

90. Rome ca. 500, showing regions, ancient monuments, old community centers,
and new basilicas

regions all were provided with the new churches, from Trastevere to the Aventine, the Viminal, the Celian, and the Campus Martius. Region I, Porta Capena, and adjoining it region XII with the Baths of Caracalla, both in the greenbelt of ancient Rome and thinly settled, were taken care of by one single church, S. Sisto Vecchio, founded by Pope Anastasius I; in region II, Caelimontium, the Celian Hill, likewise in the greenbelt, at roughly that time SS. Giovanni e Paolo was built by the rich Pammachius. S. Pudenziana from about 390 on served the inhabitants of region V, the Esquiline; S. Pietro in Vincoli, those of region III, the Oppian Hill. S. Vitale ministered to the people of region VI on the Quirinal and Viminal and in the separating valley, along the *vicus longus*; S. Anastasia, to those of region XI, Circus Maximus, at the foot of the Palatine. In the Campus Martius, region IX, S. Marco served the southern part, down to the densely settled riverbank near the bridges; S. Lorenzo in Damaso took care of the western sector; the northern part was serviced by S. Lorenzo in Lucina, built between 432 and 440. S. Marcello, east of the Corso, of about the same date, would have belonged to region VI, *via lata*, while region VII, *alta semita*, on the Quirinal, was provided for, not by a newly built church, but by the impressive fourth-century reception hall of a great mansion, the *titulus Caii*, now incorporated into the church of S. Susanna. On the Aventine, region XIII, in the greenbelt like regions I, II, III, and VII, rose S. Sabina, Peter the Illyrian's foundation. Finally, densely populated Trastevere, region XIV, had been served ever since the first half of the fourth century by two churches, S. Crisogono and S. Maria in Trastevere, presumably along with quite a few *domus ecclesiae*, led by the *titulus Caeciliae* installed in a large mansion. It is hard to believe that distribution could have happened by accident. Rather, it smacks of bureaucratic planning—a building program extended over some sixty years which appears to have assigned the new churches nearly alike to thinly and densely settled parts of town, one or sometimes two or three to a region (see below, fig. 97).

Clearly the intention in erecting these new basilicas was to replace old community centers by what might be called parish churches, capable of holding congregations far larger than the former could ever have accommodated. Still, the number of such parish churches built in Rome in the century following Constantine's death, while large in proportion to the known number of *domus ecclesiae*, is amazingly small when set against the probable size of the total Roman congregation: a bare eleven, offering space for no more than ten thousand. Even adding the roughly seven or eight thousand faithful the Lateran cathedral and St. Peter's together would hold, it was an astonishingly limited provision for a population, Christian by now, of a few hundred thousand. The larger part of the community must have still frequented community centers. Of these there must have been in the fourth and perhaps fifth centuries more than twenty-five, *pace* the figure given by the sixth-century compiler of the *Liber Pontificalis*, and probably more than the twenty-nine whose clergy attended the Roman synod of 499.[8] As much, then, as to provide additional space for larger congregations and to intensify pastoral care, the new basilicas were meant to claim public standing for the Church. To be sure, by the early fifth century the position of the Church as a public institution was no longer in doubt. By then the See of Rome, as represented by its bishop, was a power of the first magnitude, among the biggest landowners from Provence to North Africa, the spiritual lodestar of the West, and, with the decline of the Empire, forced to fill a power vacuum throughout Italy and Western Europe. *De facto*, if not *de iure*, the Roman bishop was the ruler of the city and of large parts of Italy. The decline of imperial power in the West after 400 strengthened his position, and the building policy of the papacy from the late fourth century through the pontificate of Sixtus III, 432–40, reflects this, their claim to rule from Rome, their Christian capital.

At the same time, as Rome became a Christian capital, the Church and her policy, including her building program, became increasingly imbued with the traditions of ancient Rome. Where clergy and congregations in Rome prior to 360–70 seem to have been indifferent, if not hostile, to the classical heritage, Christian leaders from the last third of the century on increasingly turned towards that past. This Romanization of Christianity, promoted by the conversion of aristocratic leaders to the Church and by the influx into the ecclesiastical hierarchy of men trained in the classical tradition, such as Pope Damasus (366–85), Ambrose, Jerome, and Augustine of Hippo, reached its peak after 400 when the last great families became Christian. Alaric's sack of Rome and the ensuing shock— "Haeret vox . . . capta est urbs quae totum cepit orbem" ("my voice fails . . . fallen has the city to which the world once fell"), writes Jerome from Bethlehem—both reinforced the position of the papacy and, by reaction, furthered its Romanization. A generation earlier, with the pontificate of Damasus, foreign-born martyrs had already acquired, as it were, posthumous Roman citizenship through having shed their blood in Rome. Peter and Paul, rather than Romulus and Remus, were the city's true founders and guardians. Classical learning and art had been shunned heretofore by Church leaders in the West because of its links with pagan gods, heroes, and myths. Now, having become innocuous through the death of paganism, antiquity was absorbed by the Roman Church in the poems of Damasus, in the lettering of his inscriptions, in the writings of Augustine, and in sarcophagi such as that of the younger Junius Bassus, which dates shortly after 359. In the planning of churches, patrons and architects strove for building on a large scale, for monumental design,

91. Rome, S. Paolo fuori le Mura, interior as of ca. 1750, engraving G. B. Piranesi

for lavish interior decoration unheard of in Rome since Constantine. At the same time, the classical tenor reached in the new churches looks back to the Hadrianic and Augustan past of Rome.[9]

The renascence in church building appears to start somewhat later than that in the figurative arts. It has its roots, it seems to me, in the last fifteen years of the fourth century with the replacement of a small Constantinian (or post-Constantinian) church over the grave of Saint Paul on the Ostian way by a basilica as large and sumptuous as that of Saint Peter on the Vatican Hill. The initiative, I submit, came from Pope Damasus as a counterstroke against the increasing strength of the pagan revival of the eighties in Rome. Whether directly or through Ambrose in Milan, he approached the ruling emperors, and they presumably decided to finance construction a year or two before 384. The basilica, completed around 400, was damaged in 441 and repaired by Pope Leo I. Thus it stood until 1823, when it burned down and was rebuilt, though in a nineteenth-century idiom, on the old plan: nave, twin aisles on either side, transept, and apse. The original structure, as repaired under Leo I, survives in descriptions, paintings, drawings, and engravings antedating the catastrophe of 1823 (fig. 91): nave colonnades, formed by homogeneous sets of shafts and capitals, all removed from older buildings, elegant stucco foliage in the arcade spandrels, murals—repainted in the thirteenth century—framed by stucco colonnettes and friezes, and a huge mosaic on the triumphal arch. Much of the decoration dated from Leo's refurbishing. But a uniform set of classical columns, mosaics perhaps in the nave arcades, and a gilded ceiling already marked the late fourth-century structure and signaled the start of a classical revival which was to grow in intensity and understanding of the classical spirit through the first half of the fifth century.[10]

As at S. Paolo fuori le Mura, homogeneous sets of splendid classical columns and capitals were carefully assembled around 400 for the building of S. Pietro in Vincoli and of S. Sabina twenty-odd years later. Finally, at S. Maria Maggiore, completed under Sixtus III between 432 and 440, the new style reaches its peak (fig. 92). Orders of fluted pilasters articulate the upper walls, corresponding to the long rows of Ionic columns below, trabeated rather than arcaded, as had been the custom for nearly a century. Figural mosaics cover the triumphal arch and once cov-

92. Rome, S. Maria Maggiore, interior

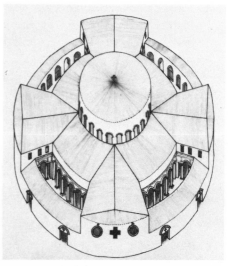

93. Rome, S. Maria Maggiore, interior, reconstruction

94. Rome, Sto. Stefano Rotondo, exterior, isometric reconstruction

95. Rome, Sto. Stefano Rotondo, interior

ered the vault of the apse, which was directly attached to it in the fifth century. (The present transept and apse were added between 1288 and 1292.) Mosaics likewise stand in each bay of the nave between the pilasters, executed in the splendid impressionistic technique that had characterized Roman painting ever since the first century and that reached its last peak in the fifth century. These nave mosaics until the end of the sixteenth century—witness contemporary drawings—were framed by gabled and colonnaded aediculae; twisted colonnettes flanked the windows, one in each bay; a classical tendril frieze, of which a small piece survives, ran atop the pilasters; and a coffered ceiling covered or was intended to cover the nave (fig. 93). Similarly, Sto. Stefano Rotondo, begun perhaps only a generation after S. Maria Maggiore, looks back, it seems to me, to models of antiquity, centuries older. The cylindrical nave, planned to be covered by a scalloped dome, the enveloping ambulatory, the four projecting tall chapels, the intervening courtyards, originally, it seems, sheltering fountains or pools and terminated by porticoes attached to the enclosing ring wall—all make for a plan in which spaces and volumes, light and shade are intertwined (figs. 94 and 95). Such planning has its root, I submit, in late Roman villa design, ultimately Hadrianic in origin, befitting the location of Sto. Stefano in the greenbelt of the Lateran quarter; the Anastasis Rotunda in Jerusalem may have served collaterally as a model. The vocabulary of Sto. Stefano likewise revived the traditions of classical building: trabeated Ionic columns, albeit crudely imitated, carry the nave wall, while in the outer zones marble pavements, stucco cornices, and traces of *opus sectile* revetment survive in fragments; the sheathing of the nave wall from the colonnade to the window zone can be reconstructed from a fifteenth-century drawing (fig. 96). Plan and decoration both, then, reflect the renascence of classical antiquity, shortlived, but representative of a papacy sure of itself and penetrated by the old educated classes, Christian by now yet conscious of the obligation to carry on the traditions of the classical past and of the grandeur of Rome.[11]

Given the new political weight of the Church both in Rome and in the world, her financial power, her amalgamation with the old Roman families, and her insistence on maintaining the classical tradition and the memories of Rome's ancient glory, the pope's residence and cathedral at the Lateran were more than ever the city's religious, political, and cultural center. But they were less than ever its topographical focus. Placed by Constantine in a quarter of elegant villas and thus never densely populated, they had always been on the outskirts of the city. By the middle of the fifth century, if not before, many of the mansions along the crest and on the slopes of the Celian Hill, from the Sessorian Palace and its church, S. Croce in Gerusalemme, to the Lateran and west to Sto. Ste-

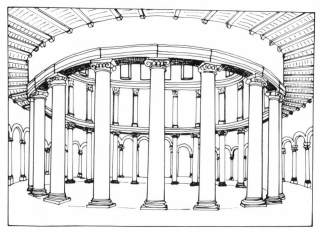

96. Rome, Sto. Stefano Rotondo, interior, reconstruction showing *opus sectile* decoration on nave wall

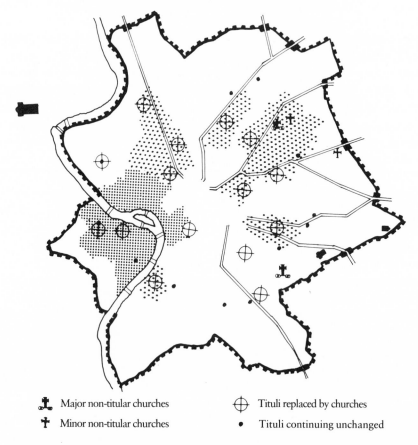

⚓ Major non-titular churches   ⊕ Tituli replaced by churches

✝ Minor non-titular churches   • Tituli continuing unchanged

97. Rome ca. 500, showing hypothetical density of settled areas and distribution of new churches

fano Rotondo and SS. Giovanni e Paolo, seem to have been abandoned. Some became church property, such as the mansion of the Valerii, turned first into a hostel and later into the convent of S. Erasmo; others remained deserted. Likewise, the stretch from the Lateran north toward the Esquiline seems to have been depopulated: two community centers in that area appear to have lost their congregations and indeed were abandoned in the course of the sixth century. Maintenance of estates grew costly, and families of means were attracted to the fleshpots of Ravenna and Constantinople and to their secure possessions in the eastern parts of the Empire, before and after the fifth-century sackings of Rome. Altogether, the population of Rome was rapidly shrinking. From perhaps 800,000 around 400, the number had dropped to 500,000 by 452, and it rapidly sank lower, to no more than 100,000 by the end of the fifth century. What was left, lived or was moving to parts of the city away from the Lateran; where exactly is hard to document, but an educated guess, based on both archaeological evidence and later development, is possible (fig. 97). The abandonment of the greenbelt—gradual, to be sure—and the resulting isolation of the Lateran were accompanied by the shrinkage of the densely inhabited area and its concentration near the river, in the bend of the Tiber and in Trastevere. Outside that *abitato*, to use a sixteenth-century term, only a few suburbs survived, two comparatively close to the Lateran: one on the Esquiline, extending perhaps as far as Via de' Selci and Via Urbana; another near the Colosseum, where S. Clemente late in the fourth century had replaced what may have been a large workshop and a small mansion given over to a Mithraic congregation. But the core of town seems to have been further west still: at the north and northwest foot of the Capitoline Hill and along the south stretch of the Corso, where tenements and warehouses installed in the third century were still in use three centuries later, and from the west cliff of the Palatine down to the river. There, the cattle market still functioned on the Forum Boarium, and, as recently as the fourth century, the tetrapylon misnamed the Janus Quadrifrons and the nearby *statio annonae* had been built, the latter the seat of the official in charge of provisioning and therefore not far from the river docks downstream. The tenements crowded on the Tiber island when the marble plan was drawn in the early third century are likely still to have been inhabited two hundred years later. There, too, as they did in the sixteenth century, three Roman bridges linked the riverbanks, leading to Trastevere, overpopulated for centuries and in the fifth century presumably still the most densely settled quarter of town. The Lateran was far away (fig. 98).[12]

  The drawbacks of so remote a site for Rome's cathedral and the residence of her bishop were evident. Being forced by circumstances into the role of both political and spiritual leader of his flock, he needed closer

contact with them than ever. The people clamored to see him and to
listen to his sermons. One thinks of Leo the Great as a political as well as
a religious preacher. He, or for that matter his predecessors, obviously
might have spoken out to his flock in any sizable church within or outside the city walls more easily accessible than the Lateran. However,
there were times when attendance at the cathedral was required of any
member of the Roman community: baptism customarily could be imparted only by the bishop, only at Easter, and only at the Lateran; and at
Christmas or Easter the community as a whole would want to gather at
the feet of their bishop in his cathedral, for many an hour's walk away.
On the other hand, moving the bishop's cathedral and his residence elsewhere inside the city—St. Peter's, one recalls, like all martyr's shrines
was outside the walls—was inconceivable; only when prevented by opposition from entering town would a pope reside and exercise his functions in a cemetery church outside the walls, as did Pope Liberius at S. Agnese. The Lateran was and remained the Roman bishop's see. It had been
established as his cathedral and residence by Constantine himself; it was
the signal monument to the triumph of the faith in the old capital and,
indeed, in the Western world. Historical sense favored retaining the old
site and its buildings, which by their very presence stressed the importance of the See of Rome. Also, for a century or more the Lateran palace

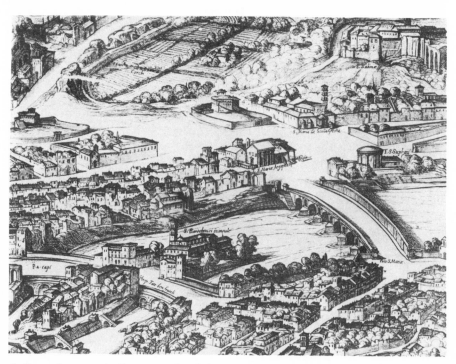

98. Rome in 1593, A. Tempesta, detail showing Tiber island and three bridges

had served the bishop and his administration well; it had been enlarged and beautified; the papal bureaucracy, one may safely assume, was comfortably installed and, with the inertia inherent in any bureaucracy, reluctant to move to new quarters. Indeed, in terms of sheer material convenience the site out there by the city walls was not too bad: airy; in the green zone, with many a mansion nearby, abandoned by the owners and fallen to the Church by donation or default; easily provisioned from fields and gardens within and beyond the walls; and with plenty of water from the nearby aqueducts—they functioned with some repairs as late as the twelfth century. It was a good place to live. Moving from the Lateran was out of the question.

However, the drawbacks inherent in the situation had to be countered: the increasing isolation of Rome's cathedral and her bishop's palace; the resulting separation of bishop and clergy from the Christian people; and the inconvenience for the latter in reaching the Lateran on great feast days, particularly for the baptismal rite at Easter, or to hear their bishop speak to them at Mass. Some of the difficulties could be overcome. Pressure on the Lateran at Easter and inconvenience for the faithful was alleviated by administering baptism at other times and places as well. Thus, by the mid-fifth century Pentecost had been set aside along with Easter as a proper time for performing it, and in urgent cases other times of the year were admitted. Concomitantly, from the late fourth century on the Roman bishop apparently also imparted baptism outside his own baptistery at the Lateran and delegated, it seems, the privilege of performing the baptismal rites to the parish clergy and those officiating at the martyrs' shrines. Hence additional baptisteries were set up in the city and at the great sanctuaries outside the walls. One had existed at the covered cemetery basilica at S. Agnese ever since Pope Liberius, then in exile, had it installed when residing there from 355 to 358, and it continued to function. St. Peter's was provided with a baptismal font by Pope Damasus—it was placed in the exedra of the north arm—and a generation later Popes Boniface and Celestine completed the decoration. Starting with the early fifth and continuing into the sixth century, baptisteries were attached to or baptismal vessels provided for a few old and a number of newly built churches both within and beyond the walls: among parish churches, at S. Anastasia, Pope Damasus's foundation, a quarter of a century after his death, between 402 and 408; at S. Vitale at roughly the same time; at S. Sabina by Pope Sixtus III, shortly after 432; at S. Lorenzo in Damaso, presumably some time after the founder's death; finally, both at S. Marcello al Corso and at S. Crisogono, where baptismal fonts of fifth-century date still exist (fig. 99). Likewise, Sixtus III rebuilt the Lateran baptistery and provided S. Maria Maggiore, as he founded it, with baptismal vessels. Finally, Leo I and Hilarus installed baptisteries

99. Rome, S. Crisogono, baptistery, reconstruction

in sanctuaries outside the walls: the former at S. Paolo and Sto. Stefano in Via Latina, the latter at S. Lorenzo fuori le Mura. The baptisteries outside the city may have been intended in the first place, though not exclusively, for the people living in the Campagna and for pilgrims, while those in town naturally would serve the resident population.[13]

Concomitantly, the construction between 380 and 450 of the large new basilicas or the conversion into churches of sizable secular halls such as S. Pudenziana seems to interlock with a liturgical innovation which came to the fore at that very time: the development of station services in the urban churches of Rome. In the fifth century these were services held at given times throughout the liturgical year at which the bishop of Rome would officiate in person on a set day in one of the city's churches, having come from the Lateran, accompanied by the clergy of the cathedral and by his administrative staff. Thus pressure was taken off the Lateran; the community of Rome did not have to come all the way there; and the bishop was enabled to meet his entire flock, albeit successively, during the season of the great festivals. As it happens, the full calendar of the station services is best known from the Middle Ages, when they were spread all over the year, mostly coinciding with the festivals of the patron saints of the station churches. Origins and early history of the stations want further study. By the fourth century they apparently had long been customary at the martyrs' shrines beyond the walls, as aliturgical prayer meetings, with or without benefit of clergy, held in the great covered cemetery basilicas—at S. Agnese or S. Lorenzo—while Mass was celebrated, it seems, at the grave in the nearby catacomb or in the basilica itself. The custom, well attested in the fourth century, continued through the fifth and sixth centuries at least. Thus, by the latter part of

the fourth century, on Christmas Day Mass was celebrated by the pope
himself at St. Peter's, as it still was a hundred years later; likewise, by the
mid-fifth century Pentecost was celebrated at St. Peter's. Within the walls,
the original and most important stational services were those in the Lateran cathedral: at Eastertide, in the fifth century the entire community of
Rome was still expected to assemble there both for aliturgical prayer
meetings and papal sermons and for the celebration of Mass during Holy
Week, except Good Friday and Easter Sunday.[14]

However, by the middle of the fifth century liturgical station services
comprising Mass were apparently customary in old and new churches
and community centers throughout the city, for between 461 and 468 Pope
Hilarus donated one large station chalice (*scyphus*) and twenty-five sets
of altar vessels "to go around the established stations. . . ." Obviously,
then, liturgical station services by that time were a matter of course,
and they were held in at least twenty-five centers of worship. The sixth-
century compiler of the *Liber Pontificalis* interpreted the number as referring "per titulos" to the twenty-five *tituli*, which he believed to have
existed in town ever since the third century. Hence the assumption that
the stations were held there at the time of Pope Hilarus; in fact, by the
fifth century a station is attested *ad duas domos*, that is, the *titulus Caii*,
S. Susanna.[15] But station services within the city were clearly not limited
to *tituli*, nor were they assigned to all of them. On the one hand, as
pointed out earlier, in the fifth century twenty-nine *tituli* were function-
ing. On the other hand, some stations at that time definitely fell to churches
outside the walls, St. Peter's for instance, others to churches in the city,
but not among the *tituli*—more of this anon—and surely quite a few of
the old community centers among the *tituli* were too small to be ser-
viceable for the large stational assemblies. However, the new basilicas
certainly were large enough, and while none would hold more than a
part of the faithful in Rome, station services held there made attendance
easier for large sectors of the population living in parts of town far distant from the Lateran and at the same time relieved pressure on the
cathedral (fig. 97).[16]

Nonetheless, the legitimate focus of the Roman community remained
at the Lateran. The cathedral and the bishop's palace were its religious
center, the seat of the papal administration and the symbol of the papacy; and the new exalted position of the Roman bishop both in the
spiritual realm and as *de facto* ruler of Rome and of large parts of Italy
made it imperative to maintain his see and enhance its splendor. Hence,
throughout the fifth century the Lateran complex was enlarged, remodeled, and redecorated. In the church, between 428 and 430 the plain gold
ground of the apse was replaced, apparently by a figural mosaic. A quarter of a century later, Leo I had the walls of the nave covered with

100. Rome, Lateran baptistery, narthex

101. Rome, Lateran baptistery, reconstruction,
1575, engraving A. Lafréri

102. Rome, Lateran, chapel of the Holy
Cross as of ca. 1500, drawing Giuliano da
Sangallo

murals, presumably a typological cycle, drawing on the Old and New Testaments—it survived into the late eighth century at least, when Pope Hadrian I referred to it in a letter to Charlemagne. Behind the basilica, Constantine's baptistery was thoroughly rebuilt by Sixtus III (432–40). It survives as remodeled again in the sixteenth and seventeenth centuries. Constantine had planned it as a simple octagon, presumably unvaulted; the outer walls, in my opinion, are still his. Eight huge columns, collected from older buildings, were to stand in the inner corners. But they were not set up by him; Sixtus placed them, not against the walls, but, as to-day, on the corners of the baptismal font in the center, carrying architraves, a second order of smaller columns, and a clerestory. Thus they delimited a central nave, surmounted probably by a scalloped dome; it was enveloped by an ambulatory, originally barrel vaulted, the walls sheathed with marble revetment and the vaulting covered with mosaic and composed, it seems, of hollow tubes. A narthex was added, terminated at either end by absidioles, its façade carried by two splendid porphyry columns (fig. 100)—shafts, capitals, bases, and frieze being spoils from some grand Roman structure. Inside the narthex, fragments of *opus sectile* on the walls and the mosaic in one of the apse vaults survive. Lafréri's reconstruction as engraved around 1560, while erroneous in the proportions, gives an approximate idea (fig. 101). The whole recalled imperial mausolea, such as S. Costanza.[17] A generation later, the adjoining chapels of St. John the Baptist and St. John the Evangelist were built and their mosaics commissioned by Pope Hilarus; and a nearby garden pavilion of second- or third-century date, cross-shaped, its convex corners concealing small octagonal alcoves, all covered with marble sheathing and mosaics, was consecrated by the same pope as a chapel of the Holy Cross, presumably to house the relic kept till then at S. Croce in Gerusalemme. The insertion of a cross into the mosaic of the main vault was enough to convert to Christian use the charming structure (fig. 102). It was torn down in 1588, but it made a deep impression on the architects of the Renaissance, and a number of their drawings still show its complex plan and its sumptuous decoration. A fountain courtyard, laid out by Hilarus, linked the chapel to the baptistery. Known only from a long description inserted into the pope's biography, it was apparently composed entirely of spoils taken from ancient buildings. But the very grandiloquence of the biographer reflects the light in which the papacy meant its buildings, and by implication itself, to be seen.[18]

If the high political and spiritual place claimed by the fifth-century popes made it imperative to clothe the Lateran with new splendor as part of their building program, another motive was the need to compete with St. Peter's. Ever since Constantine a conflict had been built into the map of Christian Rome. He had established by imperial fiat the Lateran in the

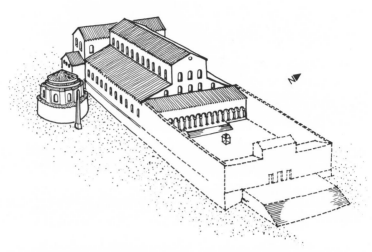

103. Rome, Old St. Peter's as of ca. 330, exterior, reconstruction

furthest southeastern corner of the city as the political, religious, and administrative center of the Christian community. Across the river, to the northwest of the city on the Vatican Hill, he had built St. Peter's basilica. Huge, larger even than the Lateran cathedral, it sheltered the shrine of the apostle and offered space for the celebration of Mass and for burial and funeral banquets (figs. 24 and 103). Situated outside the walls, it was yet easily accessible from the city by the bridge at Hadrian's mausoleum, Ponte S. Angelo. Long before Constantine, Romans and pilgrims from afar had gone to pray at the grave of Saint Peter, as they went to the graves of the other great martyrs. Indeed, his shrine and, as soon as built, his basilica overtook all other martyrs' sanctuaries of Rome in riches and importance. In ever larger numbers through the fourth and fifth centuries and beyond, the faithful flocked there to heap gifts upon it and to beg for salvation. Mausolea crowded about, among them by 400 that of the Western imperial dynasty. The Christian people of Rome never had taken and never did take to the Lateran. As a *popular* religious center, St. Peter's by far outdid their cathedral, and increasingly the Vatican basilica competed with the official focus of Christian Rome and the seat of the papacy. On the Peutinger map as brought up to date in the early fifth century, the hallmark of Rome is the basilica *ad s̄cum Petrum*, just as the Column of Constantine-Helios is the hallmark of Constantinople (fig. 104).[19] The inherent conflict and the resulting claims for primacy by each competitor, both built by Constantine—St. Peter's the popular usurper, as it were, rivaling the legitimate but not so popular cathedral at the Lateran—grew stronger during the Middle Ages. The popes of the Renaissance tried to settle it by moving to the Vatican, but it has never died. To the popes of the fifth century the built-in clash of claims must

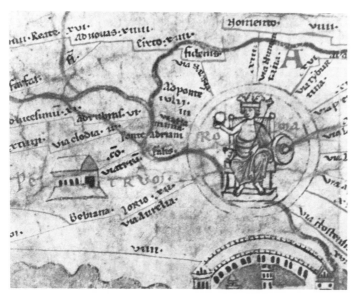

104. *Roma*, personified and marked by representation of Old St. Peter's, *Tabula Peutingeriana*, detail

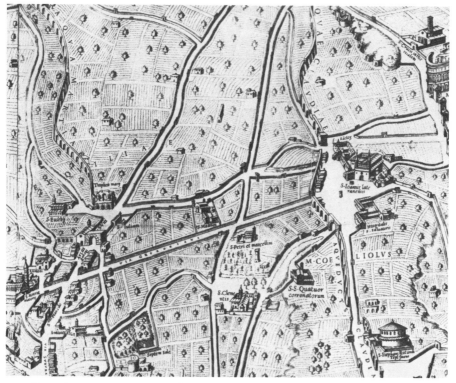

105. Rome in 1576, M. Cartaro, detail showing Lateran, S. Croce in Gerusalemme, S. Maria Maggiore, and Sto. Stefano Rotondo

have been evident, and a reaffirmation of their seat at the Lateran as the official center of Christian Rome as against the popular center at the Vatican would have seemed more than necessary.

However, the papacy reached further out, it seems, in reaffirming the Lateran's place and making it the true center of its capital. Looking at the map of Rome, one notices four churches, three founded in the fifth century and all four located between half a mile and a mile from the La teran on the perimeter of a triangle: to the north S. Maria Maggiore, to the northeast S. Bibiana, to the west Sto. Stefano Rotondo, and to the east S. Croce in Gerusalemme. The first was built or completed by Six tus III; S. Bibiana and Sto. Stefano were built between 468 and 483 by Pope Simplicius or possibly by his predecessor; S. Croce in Gerusa lemme, of course, is Helena's palace church. The fifth-century church of S. Bibiana has disappeared; the present one, remodeled by Bernini, is small and of thirteenth-century date; sixteenth-century maps no longer show it. But the others survive (fig. 105) and stand out among Roman churches by their size, by their location, and by their status. S. Maria Maggiore and Sto. Stefano are nearly twice as large as any of the parish churches built at that time; while the largest of the *tituli* basilicas, S. Sa bina, holds at best 1,400 people at services, S. Maria Maggiore accom modates close to 2,000, and Sto. Stefano (counting only nave and ambu latory), nearly 3,500, almost as many as the Lateran basilica. Clearly these churches were meant to offer space to extraordinarily large con gregations, approaching in size the crowds at the Lateran; they were intended for services, then, celebrated *tutta Roma presente* rather than for the congregation of a single parish. Only S. Croce, not being newly built for the purpose, is smaller. Likewise, they stood apart in status. No presbyter *Sanctae Mariae Maioris* or *Sancti Stefani in Caelio Monte* at tended the synods of 499 and 595; nor, incidentally, was S. Croce in Ge rusalemme, Helena's church not far from the Lateran, represented at these meetings, as were all *tituli*.[20] Apparently, then, S. Maria Maggiore, Sto. Stefano Rotondo, and S. Croce were not parish churches. They had no clergy of their own and no resident congregation. Presumably they were serviced from the Lateran by the pope or his delegate. Given their size, it looks as if they had been laid out or, in the case of S. Croce in Gerusalemme, utilized as station churches for the great feast days: Christ mas vigil at S. Maria Maggiore; Good Friday at S. Croce in Gerusa lemme; the day after Christmas, December 26, the anniversary of St. Ste phen, at Sto. Stefano Rotondo. Some of the sets of altar vessels donated by Pope Hilarus would have been intended for these services. Precise information on the location of these feast day stations, to be sure, starts only with the sixth century when, indeed, Christmas early Mass (at cock's crow rather than midnight) took place at S. Maria Maggiore and Good

Friday services at S. Croce. But, as Monseigneur Duchesne used to point out, there is such a thing as good horse sense applicable also to the history of liturgy. It is only reasonable to assume that Christmas vigil was celebrated at S. Maria Maggiore from the time it was dedicated to the Virgin by Sixtus III. The mosaics of the apse arch relate to Christ's revealing himself in the flesh and to his youth. The apse mosaic showed the *Theotokos* flanked by martyrs, and the prayers for the Christmas vigil collected in the earliest sacramentary surviving, the *Veronense*, make sense only if offered in a church dedicated to her.[21] Similarly, Good Friday was celebrated, I submit, by the fifth century if not before, at S. Croce in Gerusalemme. The church had housed a relic of the True Cross, as the *Liber Pontificalis* asserts, ever since the days of Constantine. By the late fourth century it was common knowledge that the relic had been brought by Helena from Jerusalem, and early in the fifth century, if not in Constantine's days, the church went simply by the name *Hierusalem*. It is only logical that Good Friday services took place there from the outset. Pope Hilarus, it seems, transferred the relic, perhaps for safekeeping, to the Lateran, where he dedicated the chapel of the Holy Cross. And from then on, it appears, it was brought on Good Friday in procession to S. Croce in Gerusalemme and adored with a ritual customary in the late fourth century at Jerusalem.[22] For Sto. Stefano Rotondo I cannot (nor can the historians of liturgy I have consulted) find any hagiographical explanation; perhaps there is none. Dare one then suggest a very mundane consideration? Pope and clergy on St. Stephen's day, December 26, must have been exhausted from having celebrated the day before at least two if not three masses within six hours at far distant points of town—at cock's crow at S. Maria Maggiore; around eight o'clock perhaps at S. Anastasia; around ten at St. Peter's. They may well have wanted a station service as close as possible to home base.[23]

Be that as it may, S. Maria Maggiore, S. Croce in Gerusalemme, and Sto. Stefano Rotondo from the fifth century on were closely linked to the Lateran. Given their extraparochial status, their lack of an independent clergy, and their position as station churches for the great festivals, they are best understood, I submit, as subsidiary cathedrals easy of access from the Lateran for the pope and his clergy, dependent on it and serviced from there. I wonder, however, whether there is not more to the placing of S. Maria Maggiore and Sto. Stefano in the fifth century and their choice, together with S. Croce in Gerusalemme, as dependencies of the Lateran. I have asked myself whether the three churches were not meant to outline the perimeter of a territory extending from the Lateran and set apart as the pope's very own part of Rome. Visitors ascending the Celian from the southeast corner of the Palatine, coming from the riverbank and Trastevere beyond, on approaching the Lateran would

106. Rome, Lateran, view as of ca. 1650, painting G. Dughet

encounter Sto. Stefano Rotondo; those from the north and northwest, by then the core of the city, would be greeted by S. Maria Maggiore; those from the east, from the Campagna roads, the Prenestina and Labicana, would pass by S. Croce in Gerusalemme. Smaller churches, convents, and other ecclesiastical institutions, in the course of the fifth century, rose along and inside the perimeter of the quarter: late in the fifth century S. Bibiana, founded by Pope Simplicius, and S. Andrea in Catabarbara, installed in a sumptuous reception hall, formerly of Junius Bassus the Elder; and around 500 S. Martino ai Monti, replacing an old community center. In the vicinity of the Lateran Palace settled the dependents of the papal court, high clergy and laymen, administrative personnel and their households. The old mansions in the neighborhood, abandoned by their former owners, offered convenient space. Nearby smaller folk would crowd, drawing their livelihood and expecting protection from the papal court and the great gentlemen in the area. It looks as if the entire southeastern sector of Rome were meant to become a new hub on the city map. Centered on the Lateran and extending in a vast arc north, west, and east, a *borgo* seems to be outlined, much as the one that some hundred years later extended from St. Peter's and the Vatican to the river. An attempt appears to be delineated to give the fifth-century map of Rome a new focus, reoriented towards the Lateran, just as later it was refocused on the Vatican, and for the same reasons. The new political center, the residence of the *de facto* ruler of Rome in the fifth century, the pope, claimed a central place on the map of the city.

The project remained abortive. The town proper, the *abitato*, withdrew ever further west, away not only from the Lateran, but from the churches on the perimeter as well, S. Maria Maggiore and Sto. Stefano. By the late sixth century, the cathedral of Rome and the papal palace rose isolated in the wasteland, the *disabitato*, far removed from the inhabited area. Thus it remained throughout the Middle Ages (fig. 106). Instead, St. Peter's on the slope of the Vatican Hill, across the Tiber beyond the opposite edge of Rome and outside the walls, grew to ever greater importance. The tomb of Saint Peter attracted pilgrims, and they in turn drew to the neighborhood innkeepers, vendors of *generi alimentari*, money changers, bankers, and notaries. The suburb, from the basilica to Castel and Ponte S. Angelo, and the quarter of town just across the river became an economic center of major importance. St. Peter's, the Vatican, and the Borgo developed into the hub onto which the city was gradually converging. By the fifteenth century, this process was complete. The map of Rome had been reversed and focused on its northwestern rather than its southeastern edge. Constantine's decision to locate the Christian center of Rome at the Lateran, forced on him by political expediency, had been corrected by the development of a living city.

Notes

Abbreviations of Frequently Cited Works

AASS	Société des Bollandistes, ed., *Acta Sanctorum . . .* (Paris and Rome, 1863–)
Alföldi, *Conversion*	A. Alföldi, *The Conversion of Constantine and Pagan Rome* (Oxford, 1948)
Arch St Lomb	*Archivio Storico Lombardo*
Atti Pont Accad	Atti della Pontificia Accademia Romana di Archeologia
BAC	*Bullettino di Archeologia Cristiana*
Beck, *Studien*	H. G. Beck, ed., *Studien zur Frühgeschichte Konstantinopels*, Miscellanea Byzantina Monacensia, 14 (Munich, 1973)
BZ	*Byzantinische Zeitschrift*
CA	*Cahiers Archéologiques*
CAC	*Congresso di Archeologia Cristiana*
CCC	A. Calderini, G. Chierici, and C. Cecchelli, *La Basilica di S. Lorenzo Maggiore in Milano* (Milan, 1951)
CEB	*Congrès d'Etudes Byzantines*
Chronicon Paschale	L. Dindorf, ed., *Chronicon Paschale*, PG 92:67ff
CIL	Akademie der Wissenschaften, Berlin, ed., Corpus Inscriptionum Latinarum
Colini, *Celio*	A. M. Colini, *Storia e Topografia del Celio nell'Antichità*, Atti Pont Accad, Memorie, 7 (Vatican City, 1944)
Corpus	R. Krautheimer et al., *Corpus Basilicarum Christianarum Romae*, 5 vols. (Vatican City, 1937–77)
CSEL	Akademie des Wissenschaften, Wien, ed., Corpus Scriptorum Ecclesiasticorum Latinorum

C Th   Th. Mommsen, ed., *Theodosiani Libri XVI*, 2 vols. (Berlin and Zurich, 1970 and 1971)

Dagron, *Constantinople*   G. Dagron, *Naissance d'une capitale: Constantinople* (Paris, 1974)

DOP   *Dumbarton Oaks Papers*

Dörries, *Selbstzeugnis*   A. Dörries, *Das Selbstzeugnis Kaiser Konstantins* (Göttingen, 1954)

Eusebius, *HE*   Eusebius, *Ecclesiastical History*, ed. K. Lake, LCL, 2 vols. (London and New York, 1926)

Eusebius, *LC*   Eusebius, Εἰς Κωνσταντῖνον Τριακονταετήρικος, *Eusebius Werke*, 1, ed. I. A. Heikel, GCS (Leipzig, 1902)

Eusebius, *VC* (Winkelmann)   Eusebius, *Vita Constantini, Eusebius Werke*, 1.1, *Über das Leben des Kaisers Konstantin*, ed. F. W. Winkelmann, GCS (Berlin, 1975)

FHG   C. Müller, *Fragmenta historicorum graecorum*, vol. 4 (Paris, 1885)

GCS   *Die Griechischen Christlichen Schriftsteller*, Akademie der Wissenschaften, ed. Berlin

ILCV   E. Diehl, ed., *Inscriptiones Latinae Christianae Veteres* (Berlin, 1925–1931; 2d ed., 1961)

Ist Mitt   *Istanbuler Mitteilungen*

JAC   *Jahrbuch für Antike und Christentum*

Janin, *Constantinople*   R. Janin, *Constantinople Byzantine* (Paris, 1964)

Janin, *Eglises*   R. Janin, *La géographie ecclésiastique de l'empire byzantin*, 1. 3. *Les églises* (Paris, 1953)

JDAI   *Jahrbuch des Deutschen Archäologischen Instituts*

Jerome, *Chronicle*   *Die Chronik des Hieronymus, Eusebius Werke*, 7, ed. R. Helm, GCS (Berlin, 1956)

Jones, *Later Roman Empire*   A. H. M. Jones, *The Later Roman Empire*, 284–602, 2 vols. (Oxford, 1973)

JRS   *Journal of Roman Studies*

JSAH   *Journal of the Society of Architectural Historians*

Kinney, 1970–71   D. Kinney, "'Capella Reginae': S. Aquilino in Milan," *Marsyas* 15 (1970–71):13ff

Kinney, 1972   D. Kinney, "The Evidence for the Dating of S. Lorenzo in Milan," *JSAH* 31 (1972):92ff

Kirsch, *Titelkirchen*   J. P. Kirsch, *Die römischen Titelkirchen im Altertum*, Studien zur Geschichte und Kultur des Altertums, 9, 1–2 (Paderborn, 1918)

Krautheimer, *Pelican*   R. Krautheimer, *Early Christian and Byzantine Ar-*

	chitecture, Pelican History of Art (Harmondsworth, 1965, 1st ed.; 1975, 2d ed.; 1979, 3d ed.)
Krautheimer, *Studies*	R. Krautheimer, *Studies in Early Christian, Medieval and Renaissance Art* (New York, 1969)
LCL	Loeb Classical Library
Lewis, 1969	S. Lewis, "Function and Symbolic Form in the Basilica Apostolorum," *JSAH* 28 (1969): 83ff
Lewis, 1973	S. Lewis, "San Lorenzo Revisited: A Theodosian Palace Church at Milan," *JSAH* 32 (1973): 197ff
Lietzmann	H. Lietzmann, *A History of the Early Church*, vols. 3 and 4, trans. B. L. Woolf (Cleveland and New York, 1964)
LP	L. Duchesne, ed., *Le Liber Pontificalis* (Paris, 1886–92; repr. 1955–57; 3d vol. ed. C. Vogel, Paris, 1957)
Lugli, *Centro*	G. Lugli, *Roma Antica, il centro monumentale* (Rome, 1946)
Lugli, *Monumenti*	G. Lugli, *I monumenti antichi di Roma e suburbio*, 4 vols. (Rome, 1931–40)
MacMullen, *Constantine*	R. MacMullen, *Constantine* (London, 1970)
Malalas	Johannes Malalas, *Chronographia* (*PG*, 97: 65ff)
MEFR	*Mélanges d'Archéologie et d'Histoire de l'Ecole française de Rome*
MEFRA	*Mélanges d'Archéologie et d'Histoire de l'Ecole française de Rome, Antiquité*
MGH AA	*Monumenta Germaniae Historica, Auctores Antiquissimi*
MGH Epp.	*Monumenta Germaniae Historica, Epistulae*
MGH SS	*Monumenta Germaniae Historica, Scriptores*
MGH SS rer. Mer.	*Monumenta Germaniae Historica, Scriptores rerum Merovingiarum*
MJBK	*Münchner Jahrbuch für Bildende Kunst*
Müller-Wiener, *Bildlexikon*	W. Müller-Wiener, *Bildlexikon zur Topographie Istanbuls* (Tübingen, 1977)
Mullus	Mullus, *Festschrift Theodor Klauser, Jahrbuch für Antike und Christentum*, Ergänzungsband, 1 (Münster, 1964)
Nash, *Dictionary*	E. Nash, *Pictorial Dictionary of Ancient Rome*, 2 vols. (London, 1961)
Notizie degli Scavi	Accademia Nazionale dei Lincei, ed., *Notizie degli Scavi*
Optatus	Optatus, *S. Optati Milevitani Libri VII*, ed. C. Ziwsa, *CSEL*, 26 (Vienna, 1893, repr. 1972)

Panégyriques Latins	*Panégyriques Latins*, 2 vols., ed. and trans. E. Galletier (Paris, 1952)
PBSR	*Papers of the British School at Rome*
PG	J. P. Migne, *Patrologiae cursus completus, Series Graeca* (Paris, n.d.)
Pianta marmorea	*La Pianta marmorea di Roma antica*, ed. G. Carettoni, A. M. Colini, L. Cozza, and G. Gatti (Rome, repr. 1960)
Piétri, *Roma Christiana*	C. Piétri, *Roma Christiana. Recherches sur l'eglise de Rome* . . . , Bibliothèque des Ecoles françaises d'Athènes et de Rome, 224 (Rome, 1976)
Philostorgius, *HE*	*Ex Ecclesiasticis Historiis Philostorgi Epitome confecta a Photio Patriarcha* (PG, 65:459ff); also *Die Kirchengeschichte des Philostorgius*, ed. J. Bidez and F. Winkelmann, GCS, 21² (Berlin, 1974)
PL	J. P. Migne, *Patrologiae cursus completus . . . Series Latina* (Paris, 1844–90, suppl. 1958–74)
PW	*Paulys Realencyclopädie der classischen Altertumswissenschaft*, ed. G. Wissowa et al. (Stuttgart, 1893–)
RAC	*Rivista di Archeologia Cristiana*
Rend Pont Accad	*Atti della Pontificia Accademia Romana di Archeologia. Rendiconti*
RIS	L. A. Muratori, ed., *Rerum Italicarum Scriptores* (Milan, 1723–54)
RM	*Mitteilungen des Deutschen Archäologischen Instituts, Römische Abteilung*
RQSchr	*Römische Quartalschrift*
Socrates, *HE*	Socrates, *Historia Ecclesiastica* (PG, 67:28ff)
Sozomenos, *HE*	Sozomenos, *Historia Ecclesiastica* (PG, 76:843ff); also *Die Kirchengeschichte des Sozomenos*, ed. J. Bidez and G. C. Hansen, GCS, 50 (Berlin, 1960)
Storia di Milano, 1	*Storia di Milano*, vol. 1, ed. A. Calderini et al. (Milan, 1953)
Theodoret, *HE*	Theodoret, *Historia Ecclesiastica* (PG, 82)
Unger, *Quellen*	F. W. Unger, *Quellen der byzantinischen Kunstgeschichte* (Vienna, 1878)
Valentini-Zucchetti	R. Valentini and G. Zucchetti, *Codice topografico della città di Roma* . . . , 4 vols., *Fonti per la Storia d'Italia* (Rome, 1940–53)
Zosimus	Zosimus, *Histoire nouvelle*, ed. F. Paschoud (Paris, 1971–)

1. Rome

1 The ideas underlying chapters 1 and 4, on Constantinian Rome and Rome as papal capital, were first outlined in my lecture "Il Laterano e Roma: topografia e politica nel quarto e quinto secolo," *Accademia Nazionale dei Lincei, Adunanze Straordinarie per il Conferimento dei premi A. Feltrinelli*, 1, fasc. 11 (Rome, 1975), pp. 231ff.

Sources frequently used in this chapter are Eusebius, *VC*; Eusebius, *HE*; and *C Th*. Several works on Constantine are also frequently referred to in this chapter: N. H. Baynes, *Constantine the Great and the Christian Church*, Proceedings of the British Academy, 15 (London, 1929); Alföldi, *Conversion*; Dörries, *Selbstzeugnis*; and MacMullen, *Constantine*. Basic for the historical background of the period is Jones, *Later Roman Empire*. For brief listings of the monuments of ancient Rome located on the Fora and in the Campus Martius, most handy are Lugli, *Monumenti*; Lugli, *Centro*; and Nash, *Dictionary*. On the *Curia senatus*, in particular, see Nash, *Dictionary*, 1:301ff; Lugli, *Centro*, pp. 131ff; and A. Bartoli, *Curia Senatus* (Rome, 1963). On the hall, now SS. Cosma e Damiano, originally perhaps the audience hall of the city prefect, and its domed vestibule, see Nash, *Dictionary*, 1:434, and 2:268, and A. K. Frazer, "Four Late Antique rotundas . . . ," *Marsyas* 11 (1962–64):81.

2 For the Minerva Medica, see M. Stettler, "St. Gereon in Köln und der sogenannte Tempel der Minerva Medica in Rom," *Jahrbuch des Römisch-Germanischen Zentralmuseums Mainz* 4 (1957):123ff; Nash, *Dictionary*, 2:127; and Lugli, *Monumenti*, 3:480ff. For the Gardens of Sallustius, see K. Lehmann-Hartleben and J. Lindros, "Il palazzo degli Orti Sallustiani," *Opuscula Archeologica* 1, fasc. 2 (1935):196ff. For the Sessorian Palace, see A. M. Colini, *Horti Spes Veteris*, Atti Pont Accad, Memorie, 8, fasc. 3 (Vatican City, 1955). For the general aspects of the greenbelt, see Colini, *Celio*, passim.

3 For the tenement house still standing at the foot of the Capitoline Hill, see Nash, *Dictionary*, 1:506ff. Further examples can be found in R. Meiggs, *Roman Ostia* (Oxford, 1973), passim. See *Pianta marmorea* for the marble plan of Rome, and Valentini-Zucchetti, 1:63ff, for the *regionaria*.

4 The quotation comes from Eusebius, *VC* 1. 39 (Winkelmann, 36): "εὐχαριστή-ριον ἀπεδίδου παραχρῆμα εὐχὴν τῷ τῆς νικῆς αἰτίῳ." The legal meanings as well as the rites connected with *inauguratio, sanctio, dedicatio*, and *consecratio* in Roman religious law are explained in L. Voelkl, *Die Kirchenstiftungen des Kaisers Konstantin im Lichte des römischen Sakralrechts*, Arbeitsgemeinschaft des Landes Nordrhein-Westfalen, 11 (Cologne and Opladen, 1964), pp. 17ff.

5 For the mansions on the Celian Hill, see Colini, *Celio*; V. Santa Maria Scrinari, "Per la storia e la topografia del Laterano," *Bollettino d'Arte* 5 (1965):38ff; and idem, "Scavi sotto Sala Manzoni all'ospedale di S. Giovanni in Roma," *Rend Pont Accad* 41 (1968–69):167ff.

6 The conjectural dating of the *dedicatio* and/or *consecratio* of the Lateran cathe-

dral here proposed is based on the following premises: the feast of the *dedicatio* on November 9, while first recorded around 1000 (P. Jounel, *Le culte des Saints dans les basiliques du Latran et du Vatican*, Collection de l'Ecole française de Rome, 26 [Rome, 1977], p. 305) is presumably much older; church dedications and consecrations—the legal difference was soon obliterated—ever since the early Middle Ages, and in all likelihood since Early Christian times, were customarily placed on Sundays; and Sunday, in Constantine's early reign, coincides with November 9 only in 312 and 318—the occurrences in 329 and 335 obviously being too late. See also *Corpus*, 5:10, 89ff, and J. Ruysschaert, "L'inscription absidiale primitive de S. Pierre," *Rend Pont Accad* 40 (1967–68): 171ff.

7 For the archeological, documentary, and visual evidence underlying our proposed reconstruction of the Constantinian basilica at the Lateran, see Corpus, 5:1ff. The principal errors of the reconstruction in Gagliardi's fresco are the substitution of arcades for the original architrave and the insertion of a transept which Constantine's church lacked—the existing one is of medieval date.

8 For the possible location of the bishop's mansion, see V. Santa Maria Scrinari, "Per la storia," and E. Nash, "Convenerunt in domum Faustae in Laterano S. Optati Milevitani, I, 123," *RQSchr* 71 (1976): 1ff.

9 For the *domus ecclesiae* at Dura-Europos, see *The Excavations at Dura-Europos, Final Report*, 8, part 2: *The Christian Building*, ed. C. Kraeling (New Haven, 1967). Another small-town *domus ecclesiae* at Cirte-Constantine in North Africa is known from the minutes of its confiscation in 305, reported by Optatus (CSEL, 26:186ff).

10 For the hall at S. Crisogono, see *Corpus*, 1:144ff, and more recently, B. M. Apollonj Ghetti, *S. Crisogono*, Le Chiese di Roma Illustrate, 92 (Rome, 1966). The hall may date from Constantine's early years. For the garden hall below S. Pietro in Vincoli, see A. M. Colini and G. Matthiae, *Ricerche intorno a S. Pietro in Vincoli*, Atti Pont Accad, Memorie, 9, fasc. 2 (Vatican City, 1966), p. 57. A *domus ecclesiae*, presumably installed in a tenement, is incorporated into the church of SS. Giovanni e Paolo and can be conjecturally reconstructed; see *Corpus*, 1:243ff.

11 R. Krautheimer, "The Constantinian Basilica," *DOP* 21 (1967): 117ff, and J. B. Ward-Perkins, "Constantine and the Origins of the Christian Basilica," *PBSR* 22 (1954): 69ff.

12 For the concept of Christ as *basileus*, see J. Kollwitz, "Das Bild von Christus dem König . . . ," *Theologie und Glaube* 38 (1947): 95ff; P. Beskow, *Rex Gloriae: The Kingship of Christ in the Early Church* (Uppsala, 1962), passim; and U. Süssenbach, *Christuskult und kaiserliche Baupolitik bei Konstantin* (Bonn, 1977), passim. The quotation is from Eusebius, *HE* 10. 4. 16 (*LCL*, 2:406).

13 Süssenbach, *Christuskult*, in my opinion overshoots the mark in ascribing to
Constantine alone the creation of the new church type and in deriving that type
from audience halls only, rather than seeing it as a new variant within the entire
genus basilica. What have been called imperial elements in Constantinian
church building (R. Stapleford, "Constantinian Politics and the Atrium
Church," in *Art and Architecture in the Service of Politics*, ed. H. A. Millon
[Cambridge, Mass., 1979], pp. 2ff) are due in my opinion less to imperial
involvement in planning than to the view of Christ as Emperor of Heaven.

14 Eusebius, *VC* 3. 3 (Winkelmann, 82).

15 For the wealth of the Church at that time, see Piétri, *Roma Christiana*, pp. 89ff.

16 For S. Lorenzo fuori le Mura, see *Corpus*, 2:1ff; for S. Agnese fuori le Mura,
F. W. Deichmann, "Die Lage der Konstantinischen Basilika der heiligen Agnes
an der Via Nomentana," *RAC* 22 (1946):1ff; for SS. Marcellino e Pietro, F. W.
Deichmann and A. Tschira, "Das Mausoleum der Kaiserin Helena und die
Basilika der heiligen Marcellinus und Petrus an der Via Labicana vor Rom,"
JDAI 72 (1957):44ff, and *Corpus*, 2:191ff (recent excavations undertaken by
the École Française have traced the outline of large porticoed courtyards flank-
ing the basilica on one, and presumably on either side); for S. Sebastiano,
Corpus, 4:99ff; for St. Peter's, *Corpus*, 5:165ff. Regarding the function
of these *coemeteria subteglata*, see R. Krautheimer, "Mensa-Coemeterium-
Martyrium," *CA* 11 (1960):15ff, as well as Krautheimer, *Studies*, 35ff. In opposition to this viewpoint is F. W. Deichmann, "Märtyrerbasilika, Martyrion,
Memoria und Altargrab," *RM* 77 (1970):144ff.

   For the palace church S. Croce in Gerusalemme, see A. M. Colini, *Horti
Spes Veteris*, and *Corpus*, 1:165ff. I see no reason to doubt the tradition of
Helena's having brought to her Roman palace the relic of the cross from her
pilgrimage to the Holy Land. That the canopy housing the relic at S. Croce was
represented about 440 on the "Pola casket" and resembled that over Christ's
tomb at Jerusalem is a suggestion on which I am happy to agree with M. Guar-
ducci, *La Capsella eburnea di Samagher*, Società Istriana di Archeologia e Storia
Patria, Atti e Memorie, n.s. 26 (Trieste, 1978), pp. 77ff.

17 On a Roman emperor's obligation to erect monumental buildings, see *Mac-
Mullen*, Constantine, p. 49; on Constantine's having done so, see *Panégyriques
Latins*, X(4)35 (Galletier, 2:195).

18 For Constantine's thermae, see Lugli, *Monumenti*, 3:307ff and Nash, *Dictionary*, 2:442ff; for the equestrian statue, the *caballus Constantini*, see the *Itine-
rarium Einsidlense* (Valentini-Zucchetti, 2:166), and Lugli, *Centro*, p. 160. For
the *basilica nova* and for the colossal statue of Constantine and its early
date, see H. Kähler, "Konstantin—313," *JDAI* 67 (1952):1ff; T. Buddensieg,
"Die Konstantinsbasilika . . . und der Marmor-Koloss Konstantins . . . ,"
MJBK, 3d ser., 13 (1962):37ff; and W. Helbig, *Führer durch die öffentlichen
Sammlungen Roms*, ed. H. Speier (Tübingen, 1966), 2:252ff, no. 1441. For the

Janus Quadrifrons, see Lugli, *Centro*, pp. 592ff. For the restoration of the Circus Maximus, see Sextus Aurelius Victor, *Liber de Caesaribus* 40. 27 (ed. F. Pichlmayr, rev. R. Gruendel [Leipzig, 1966], p. 124); *Panégyriques Latins*, X(4) 35 (Galletier, 2:195); Lugli, *Centro*, pp. 599ff; and Nash, *Dictionary*, 1:236ff.

19 H. v. Schönebeck, *Beiträge zur Religionspolitik des Maxentius und Konstantin*, Klio, Beiheft 43 (Wiesbaden, 1939; reprint ed., Aalen, 1969), pp. 87ff, followed by Alföldi, *Conversion*, pp. 50ff, had anticipated my explanation of the political reasons underlying the remote location of the Lateran, as I discovered after having worked out the problem myself.

The interpretation of the sources with regard to Constantine's policies can obviously be my own only to a small degree. It is based on and coincides for the greater part with those of Alföldi, *Conversion*; MacMullen, *Constantine*; J. Straub, *Vom Herrscherideal in der Spätantike* (Stuttgart, 1939; reprint ed., 1964); and idem, "Konstantins christliches Sendungsbewusstsein," in *Regeneratio Imperii* (Darmstadt, 1972), pp. 70ff, originally published in *Das neue Bild der Antike* 2 (1942): 374ff.

20 On *opera publica*, see *C Th*, XV, and Jones, *Later Roman Empire*, pp. 461ff and passim. On the *res privata*, see ibid., pp. 411ff, 732ff, and passim, also A. Masi, *Ricerche sulla res privata del princeps*, Università di Cagliari, Pubblicazioni della Facoltà di Giurisprudenza 1, fasc. 2 (Milan, 1971).

21 For gifts from the *res privata*, see also R. MacMullen, "Two Notes on Imperial Properties," *Athenaeum*, n.s. 54 (1976): 19ff. Property of the fisc was used in Cirte-Constantine in 330; see Optatus (CSEL, 26:213ff).

22 For the permission of the Senate for the use of *opera publica* at S. Paolo fuori le Mura, see *Epistulae Imperatorum Pontificum* . . . (CSEL, 35) ed. O. Günther (Vienna, 1895), pp. 46ff. Eusebius, *HE* 10. 5. 10 (LCL, 2:450), quoting the Milan decree, calls the receiving body τὸ σῶμα τῶν χριστιανῶν," obviously translated from *corpus Christianorum*, while *C Th*, XVI, 2. 4 (July 3, 321) refers to the "catholicae [ecclesiae] venerabile consilium."

23 For the inscription on the gold cross at St. Peter's, see *LP*, 1:180, and R. Egger, "Das Goldkreuz am Grabe Petri," *Oesterreichische Akademie der Wissenschaften, Phil.-Hist. Klasse, Anzeigen*, (1959), pp. 181ff. For what was expected of imperial buildings, see MacMullen, *Constantine*, p. 49.

24 Eusebius, *VC* 1. 32 (Winkelmann, 31ff).

25 On the Sun as the emperor's Divine Companion, see Baynes, *Constantine*, pp. 95ff; A. D. Nock, "The Emperor's Divine Comes," *Journal of Roman Studies* 37 (1947): 102ff; and E. Kantorowicz, "Oriens Augusti—Lever du Roi," *DOP* 17 (1963): 117ff; also Panegyric VIII (5) 14, *Panégyriques Latins* (Galletier, 2:102), as pointed out by E. Faure, "Notes sur le panégyrique VIII," *Byzantion*

31 (1961): 1ff, especially p. 33. The god's appearance to Constantine in 310 is
mentioned in *Panégyriques Latins*, VII (6) 21 (Galletier, 2:72). For the representation of Sol on Constantine's coin of 325, see M. R. Alföldi, "Die Sol
Comes-Münze vom Jahre 325. Neues zur Bekehrung Constantins," Mullus, pp.
10ff, superseding P. Bruun, "The Disappearance of Sol from the Coins of Constantine," *Arctos*, n.s. 2 (1958), pp. 15ff, and his dating of the latest Sol coins
in 321.

26 On the promotion of Christians at court, see Optatus (CSEL, 26, app. 3, pp.
204ff); on the role of bishops, Eusebius, *VC* 1. 32 (Winkelmann, 31); and on
the exemption of the clergy from public service, Eusebius, *HE* 10. 7. 1 (LCL,
2:462ff), confirmed by *C Th*, XVI, 2. 1 (October 3, 313).

27 Quotations are from *Panégyriques Latins*, IX (12) 4 and 26, and X (4) (Galletier, 2:124, 144 and 172). For vague formulae used to denote the Deity, see
also Eusebius, *VC* 2. 12 (Winkelmann, 53); MacMullen, *Constantine*, p. 841;
Alföldi, *Conversion*, pp. 132ff; and J. Straub, "Constantine as ʽκοινὸς
ἐπίσκοπος,'" *DOP* 21 (1967): 37ff, especially pp. 41ff.
   The expression *instinctu divinitatis* in the inscription on the Arch of Constantine is interpreted by H.-P. L'Orange, *Der spätantike Bildschmuck des Kon-
stantinsbogen* (Berlin, 1939), pp. 176ff, as a straightforward and exclusive
reference to the pagan divinities appearing in the reliefs, primarily to *Sol Invictus*, and I think it quite possible that the pagans in the Senate viewed the term
that way; see also H. Lietzmann, "Der Glaube Konstantins des Grossen," *Sitzungsberichte der Preussischen Akademie der Wissenschaften, Philosophisch-
historische Klasse*, Berlin, 1937), pp. 263ff. But I still hold with the opinion,
indicated by G. De Rossi, "L'iscrizione dell'Arco trionfale di Constantino,"
BAC 1 (1863): 57ff, that the term was ambiguous and, I would add, intention-
ally chosen.

28 Alföldi, *Conversion*, pp. 61ff; see also *Panégyriques Latins*, IX (12) 19, (Galletier, 2:138f), and Eusebius, *VC* 1. 40 (Winkelmann, 36ff). On the dream, see
Eusebius, *VC* 1. 29 (Winkelmann, 30), and Lactantius, *De mortibus per-
secutorum*, 44 (CSEL, 26, 2. 2, pp. 223ff). On the labarum and its miracle-
working powers, see Eusebius, *VC* 1. 30, and 2. 7–9 (Winkelmann, 30ff and
50ff), also Eusebius, *LC* 9. 8 (Heikel, 220). On Christian attitudes towards the
old gods, see Eusebius, *VC* 1. 27, and 2. 3 (Winkelmann, 28ff and 48ff). On
Constantine's early approach to Christianity, see Eusebius, *VC* 1. 32 (Winkelmann, 31ff); the quotation is from Alföldi, *Conversion*, p. 21.

29 On Constantine's recollection of his conversion, see Eusebius, *VC* 1. 30ff and
passim (Winkelmann, 30ff). The quotation is from MacMullen, *Constantine*,
pp. 110ff.

30 For Constantine's avoidance of the ritual visit to *Jupiter Capitolinus* on his
triumphal entry into Rome as early as 312, see J. Straub, "Konstantin's Verzicht
auf den Gang zum Kapitol," *Historia* 4 (1955): 297ff, based on *Panégyriques*

Latins IX (12) 19 (Galletier, 2:138f). F. Paschoud, "Zosimus 2.29 . . . ," *Historia* 20 (1971):334ff, places that break with the customary ceremonial at the celebration of Constantine's decennalia in 315.

31 On Constantine's attitudes toward paganism, see J. Straub, "Constantine as κοίνὸς ἐπίσκοπος." The laws quoted are *C Th*, IX, 16. 1 and 2 (February 1 and May 15, 319).

On the sabbath law, see *C Th*, II, 8. 1 (July 3, 321). On the *flamines* of the *gens Flavia*, see Sextus Aurelius Victor, *Liber de Caesaribus* 40. 28, p. 124. On the shrine at Spello, see CIL 11. 2. 5265, as quoted in Dörries, *Selbstzeugnis*, pp. 209ff, following L. Bréhier and P. Battifol, *Les survivances du culte impérial* (Paris, 1920), p. 14. On Constantine's retaining the title of *Pontifex Maximus*, see CIL 5. 8004, 8412, and 10059; cf. Dörries, *Selbstzeugnis*, pp. 216ff.

Remains of a wish to spare pagan feelings by the frequent use of vague terms in referring to the Deity—τὸ Θεῖον, τὸ κρεῖττον—seem to intrude as late as 324 into the letter addressed to the *provinciales* of the Eastern provinces; see Eusebius, *VC* 2. 24ff (Winkelmann, 58ff).

32 Constantine's strictly orthodox *Oratio ad sanctorum coetum* has recently been assigned a date as early as 317 rather than 325 by T. D. Barnes, "The Emperor Constantine's Good Friday Sermon," *Journal of Theological Studies* 27 (1976):414ff, as kindly pointed out to me by P. Brown; the proposal wants further verification.

33 Eusebius, *VC* 1. 36 and 39 (Winkelmann, 33ff and 36).

34 On the trophy with the Chi-Rho, see Eusebius, *VC* 1. 40 (Winkelmann, 36); on the gilded statue of Constantine set up by the Senate, see *Panégyriques Latins* IX (12) 25 (Galletier, 2:143) and Chr. Ligota, "Constantiniana," *Journal of the Warburg and Courtauld Institutes* 26 (1963):178ff; on this (or a second?) statue's being provided by Constantine with the labarum (or a Chi-Rho) and a changed inscription, see Eusebius, *HE* 9. 9. 10ff (LCL 2:362ff); see also Alföldi, *Conversion*, pp. 64 and 132, n. 23, and Ligota, "Constantiniana," pp. 185ff. On Constantine's claim to have freed and restored the Senate and People of Rome through the sign of salvation, see Eusebius, *HE*, as quoted; on the intimated provocation of non-Christians, see Eusebius, *HE* 10. 4. 16 (LCL, 2:406ff).

35 The date of the colossal head from the Basilica Nova is still a topic of contention. The early dating, first proposed by H. Kähler, "Konstantin—313," and sustained by H. von Heintze, in W. Helbig, *Führer durch die öffentlichen Sammlungen Roms*, 2 vols., ed. H. Speier (Tübingen, 1966), 2:252ff, no. 1441, is more convincing to me than a late date, as given in R. Delbrück, *Spätantike Kaiserporträts* (Berlin and Leipzig, 1933), pp. 121ff, and proposed again by E. Harrison, "The Constantinian Portrait," *DOP* 21 (1967):79ff, especially pp. 94ff, and J. Breckenridge, in *The Age of Spirituality . . . Catalogue*, ed. K. Weitzmann (New York, 1979), pp. 18ff. On the site of the find, the west apse

of the basilica, see T. Buddensieg, "Die Konstantinsbasilika." The reference to Trajan was pointed out to me by David Wright.

36 On coins honoring Senate and *equites*, see Alföldi, *Conversion*, pp. 64 and 99ff; on the medallion of 315, see M. Alföldi, *Die Constantinische Goldprägung* (Mainz, 1963), pp. 41ff. On the attempted winning over of the old guard, see Alföldi, *Conversion*, pp. 61ff.

37 On Constantine's restriction of sacrifices at the celebration of his decennalia, see Eusebius, *VC* 1. 48 (Winkelmann, 40). The decrees regarding *haruspices* are *C Th*, IX, 16. 1 and 2 (February 1 and May 15, 319) and XVI, 10. 1 (December 17, 320–21).

38 Decrees favoring the clergy starting as early as 313 and continuing through 330 are scattered through *C Th*, XVI: XVI, 2. 1 (October 31, 313[?]; XVI, 2. 2 (October 21, 319); XVI, 2. 3 (July 18, 320); XVI, 2. 5 (May 25, 323); XVI, 2. 5 (June 1, 326); XVI, 5. 1 (September 1, 326); and XVI, 2. 7 (February 5, 330). Moreover, there is a rescript to the governor of North Africa, prior to October 313 (Eusebius, *HE* 10. 7. 1 [LCL, 2:465] and Optatus [CSEL, 26:213ff]) and a letter addressed February 15, 330, to the bishops of Numidia. The large number of decrees concerning the African provinces is obviously linked to the suppression of the Catholics by the Donatists. Finally, a decree of July 3, 321 (*C Th*, XVI, 2. 4) permits legacies to the Church—a decisive privilege.

On the date of Constantine's "Speech to the Assembly of Saints," see T. D. Barnes, "The Emperor Constantine's Good Friday Sermon."

39 On the painting of Constantine in heaven, see Eusebius, *VC* 4. 65 (Winkelmann, 146ff); for similar notions, see CIL 6. 1151 and 1152; 8. 4414, as quoted by Dörries, *Selbstzeugnis*, pp. 216ff.

40 Alföldi, *Conversion*, p. 50.

II. Constantinople

1 Basic for this chapter are: for the sources regarding the monuments, Janin, *Constantinople*; for monuments surviving, Müller-Wiener, *Bildlexikon*; for the historical sources and their interpretation, Dagron, *Constantinople*; and for a number of general and detailed questions, Beck, *Studien*, passim. Still useful, though more than a hundred years old, for the city and its public buildings, is the collection of sources (in German translation), Unger, *Quellen*.

2 "ἕνα , . . τὸν ἔπι πάντων Θεὸν . . . ἕνα δὲ τὸν μονογένα σωτῆρα . . . ἕνα δὲ καὶ ἔπι γῆς διοΘωρτὴν βασιλέα . . ." (Eusebius, *LC* 10 [Heikel, 223; *PG*, 20:1373]).

3 For Constantine's itineraries, see *C Th*, I and CCIXff, and P. M. Bruun, *Studies*

in Constantinian Chronology (New York, 1961), pp. 102ff. For pleas for him to return to Rome, see Nazarius, Panegyric X (4) 38, *Panégyriques Latins* (Galletier, 2:198). For his refusal to attend sacrifices on the Capitol, see above, chapter 1, note 30.

4 *C Th*, I and CCXIIff and Alföldi, *Conversion*, p. 75, n. 2, quoting *Anon. Cont. Dionysi, FHG*, 4:199.

5 The date of foundation, as generally accepted, is based on Themistios, *Oratio* 4 (ed. H. Schenkel and G. Downey [Leipzig, 1964], p. 83), where that event is made to coincide with the nomination of Constantius to the rank of Caesar. One proposed date for the nomination is November 8, 324: see O. Seeck, *Regesten der Kaiser und Päpste* (Stuttgart, 1919), p. 174; J. Moreau, "Nachträge zum Reallexikon für Antike und Christentum," *JAC* 2 (1959):158ff, based on *Consularia Constantinopolitana* (*MGH AA*, 9, *Chronica Minora*, 1:232), with an erroneous reference to Constantine II, and on *Chronicon Paschale* (ibid. and *PG*, 92:704ff), with erroneous references to the year 325, to Constans, rather than Constantius, and to the celebration of Constantine's vicennalia in Rome in 325. Alternatively, the nomination of Constantius may have fallen on November 13, 324, as witness an inscription from Amiternum (*Notizie degli Scavi*, 1936, pp. 96ff). I cannot find any confirmation for the date November 3, 324 given by Jones, *Later Roman Empire*, p. 1081, n. 12; he refers to *Chronica Minora*, 1:232 and 643 (cited above), but these passages provide no corresponding date. However, A. Alföldi, "A Few Notes on the Foundation of Constantinople," *JRS* 37 (1946):10ff, especially n. 9 (the reference to Constantine II is an obvious *lapsus calami*) points out that the linking by Themistios of the city's foundation and of Constantius' promotion need not mean that they actually took place on the same day. If I had to choose between November 8 and November 13, I would prefer the former, which fell on a Sunday in 324.

6 The quotation is from *Excerpta Valesiana* 6. 30, in *Ammianus Marcellinus*, ed. J. C. Rolfe, LCL, 3:506ff, 526). See also Dagron, *Constantinople*, for a more, perhaps too, far-reaching interpretation.

7 For the *sanctio* (*limitatio*), see Philostorgius, *HE* 2. 9 (*GCS*, 20ff; *PG*, 65:472). For the rite in its earliest form, see L. Voelkl, *Die Kirchenstiftungen des Kaisers Konstantin im Lichte des römischen Sakralrechts*, Arbeitsgemeinschaft des Landes Nordrhein-Westfalen, 11 (Cologne and Opladen, 1964), p. 17. For the consultation of pagan religious leaders, perhaps in their quality as augurs or astrologers, see Johannis Laurentii Lydi, *Liber de Mensibus* 4. 2 (ed. R. Wünsch [Leipzig, 1898], pp. 65ff): "ὁ δὲ Πραιτέξτατος ὁ ἱεροφάντης ὁ Σωπάτρῳ τε τῷ τελεστῇ καὶ Κωνσταντίνῳ . . . σνλλαβὼν ἐπὶ τῷ πολίσμῳ τῆς εἰδαίμονος ταύτης πόλεως. . . ." On Sopatros, see *PW*, 3 (ser. 2. 5):1006ff; on Praetextatus see, most recently, L. Cracco Ruggini, *Il paganesimo romano tra religione e politica*, Accademia Nazionale dei Lincei, Memorie, Classe scienze morali, storiche e filologiche, ser. 8, 23, fasc. 1 (Rome, 1977), passim, especially pp. 131ff.

S. Mazzarino, *Antico, Tardo-antico . . .* , (Bari, 1974), 1:122ff, places the *inauguratio* in 324, the *dedicatio* in 328, the *consecratio* in 330; see also L. Cracco Ruggini, *Il paganesimo romano*, pp. 138ff.

For a foundation date of H. Sophia ca. 326, see *Chronicon Paschale*, Ol. 285, 1 (360) (*PG*, 92:737), calculating back "μίκρῳ πρόσῳ" thirty-four years from the consecration on February 15, 360. I did not take that statement seriously enough when assigning the start of construction at H. Sophia to a time after Constantine's death (unfortunately still Krautheimer, *Pelican*³, p. 486, n. 27). For the date 328 and for the building of the walls and other constructions, see *Chronicon Paschale*, Ol. 277, 1 (328) (*PG*, 92:708).

8 For the mint's starting in 326, prior to Crispus's death, see P. M. Bruun, *Constantinian Chronology*, p. 67, and P. M. Bruun, ed., *The Roman Imperial Coinage*, 7 (London, 1968), pp. 562ff; for the Tychē coin, see ibid., p. 564 and n. 53.

9 For the date of Constantine's decision to make Constantinople his capital, see Bruun, *Imperial Coinage*, 7, 563:327. For the character of the city as a *Großstadt*, see H. G. Beck, "Großstadt-Probleme . . . ," in Beck, *Studien*, pp. 1ff, especially pp. 4ff. For Constantine's dedication decree, see Socrates, *HE* 1. 16 (*PG*, 67:116), and Hesychios, *Patria* 39, in *Scriptores Originum Constantinopolitanarum*, ed. Th. Preger (Leipzig, 1901), p. 16. For the relation of Constantinople to Rome, see Jones, *Later Roman Empire*, p. 83, and, in particular, Dagron, *Constantinople*, pp. 43ff, 53ff, and passim.

10 For the site of Greek Byzantium, see Janin, *Constantinople*, pp. 11ff, and Müller-Wiener, *Bildlexikon*, pp. 16ff; for the wall and harbor, Janin, *Constantinople*, pp. 16ff, and Müller-Wiener, *Bildlexikon*, p. 18; for the gate, ibid., pp. 167, 169; for the earlier hippodrome, the Baths of Zeuxippos, and the porticoed square, Janin, *Constantinople*, p. 171 and passim, and Müller-Wiener, *Bildlexikon*, pp. 17ff, 51, and 64; for other administrative buildings, Malalas, *Chronographia* 13 (*PG*, 97:484).

11 On the Walls of Theodosius II, see F. Krischen, *Die Landmauer von Konstantinopel*, 1 (Berlin, 1938); B. Meyer-Plath and A. M. Schneider, *Die Landmauer von Konstantinopel*, 2 (Berlin, 1943); Müller-Wiener, *Bildlexikon*, pp. 286ff. On the aqueduct(s), see Janin, *Constantinople*, pp. 189 and 201ff, and Müller-Wiener, *Bildlexikon*, p. 175. On provisioning and shipping laws, see *C Th*, XIII, 5. 5 (September 18, 326), and XIII, 5. 7 (December 1, 334). On the new harbor and warehouse, see Beck, *Studien*, p. 6 and Janin, *Constantinople*, pp. 225ff. On the shoddy quality of construction, see, e.g., Zosimus 2. 32 (Paschoud, 105). On mansions and the income attached to them, see Anonymous Valesianus, *Excerpta Valesiana* 6. 30; Sozomenos, *HE* 2. 3. 4 (*GCS*, 50, 52; PG, 67:957); *C Th, Theodosiani Novellae*, nov. 5, sec. 1. On houses and the free bread distribution linked to them (rather than to individuals), see *C Th*, XIV, 17. 12 (November 20, 393, when revoked). The privileges are summed up by Dagron, *Constantinople*, pp. 520ff. On population estimates, see D. Jacoby, "La popula-

tion de Constantinople à l'époque byzantine . . . ," *Byzantion* 31 (1961): 81ff, especially p. 96.

12 For H. Eirene as cathedral, see Socrates, *HE* 1. 16. 37; 2. 6. (*PG*, 67: 116, 195ff); for its status as co-cathedral, ibid. 2. 16 (*PG*, 67: 217), also Janin, *Eglises*, pp. 1081ff.; for Justinian's rebuilding of the old H. Eirene, U. Peschlow, *Die Irenenkirche in Konstantinopel* (Berlin, 1978).

13 On the layout of the Severan town, see Janin, *Constantinople*, p. 911, and Müller-Wiener, *Bildlexikon*, p. 269. On Constantine's remodeling of preexisting elements, see W. Müller-Wiener, review of M. Restlé, *Reclams Kunstführer, Istanbul, Bursa, Edirne, Iznik,* (Stuttgart, 1976), in *BZ* 72 (1979): 106ff: "Was in der konstantinischen Bauphase . . . geschah, war einerseits die zweckmässige . . . Ausnutzung der . . . geographischen Voraussetzungen, zum anderen der Ausbau alter Verkehrswege: die Anlage der vier emboloi war im Grunde nur der monumentale Ausbau der . . . existierenden Strassen. Ergänzend kamen dazu Nord–Süd Verbindungen. . . . Eine Planung . . . im 4. Jahrhundert hat es sicher gegeben . . . die grossen Säulenstrassen waren die Planungsachsen. . . . dahinter mag sich . . . Gassengewirr versteckt haben."
    The quotation from Jerome, *Chronicle*, 232, under the year 330, probably concerns both statuary and precious building materials.

14 For antique statuary reused, see Janin, *Constantinople*, pp. 59ff, 155f, and passim; C. Mango, "Antique Statuary and the Byzantine Beholder," *DOP* 17 (1963): 53ff; Dagron, *Constantinople*, pp. 139f. For the hippodrome, see Müller-Wiener, *Bildlexikon*, pp. 64ff; R. Guilland, *Etudes de topographie de Constantinople byzantine,* (Berlin [East], 1969), 1: 369ff. On the role of the hippodrome, see Dagron, *Constantinople*, pp. 320ff. The view of the hippodrome, engraved in 1580, hence posthumously, and published in O. Panvinio, *De ludis circensibus* (Venice, 1600), was apparently drawn on the spot and is accompanied, in the same work, pp. 61f, by a detailed description with measurements, obviously furnished by an eyewitness. The absence of mosques from the engraving and joined to this the presence on the spina of a number of objects no longer existing in the sixteenth century suggests a fifteenth-century date for the original on which it is based. Panvinio was never in Constantinople (see D. A. Perini, *Onofrio Panvinio e le sue opere* [Rome, 1899]).

15 On the palace, see Janin, *Constantinople*, pp. 106ff; R. Guilland, *Topographie,* pp. 1ff; also R. Krautheimer, "Die Decanneacubita in Konstantinopel," in *Tortulae, RQSchr,* suppl., 30 (1966), pp. 195ff. For the site, see Müller-Wiener, *Bildlexikon*, p. 229.

16 Eusebius, *VC* 3. 3 (Winkelmann, 82); A. Grabar, *L'empereur dans l'art Byzantin* (Paris, 1936), pp. 34f, 43f.

17 For the consecration date, 360, of H. Sophia, see *Chronicon Paschale*, Ol. 285, 1 (360) (*PG*, 92: 736f). For the remains of Constantine's church and its fifth-

century successor, see A. M. Schneider, *Die Grabung im Vorhof der Sophien-kirche*, Istanbuler Forschungen, 12 (Berlin, 1941); F. W. Deichmann, *Studien zur Architektur Konstantinopels* (Baden-Baden, 1956), pp. 63ff; and Müller-Wiener, *Bildlexikon*, pp. 84ff.

The reconstruction of the fifth-century church as proposed by W. Kleiss, "Beobachtungen an der Haghia Sophia in Istanbul," *Ist Mitt* 15 (1965):168ff, especially fig. 5, is erroneous. See Th. Mathews, *The Early Churches of Constantinople* (University Park, Pa., and London, 1971), p. 19.

18 See Eusebius, *VC* 3. 29–39 (Winkelmann, 97ff) for the description. My own reconstruction can be found in Krautheimer, *Pelican*[1], fig. 16; ibid.[2], fig. 27A; ibid.[3], revised, pp. 62ff and fig. 27A, B, C. See ibid., pp. 62ff and 488ff, n. 45, with bibliography, on the complex on Golgotha; on the breadmold (Cleveland Museum) see now also K. Weitzmann, ed., *The Age of Spirituality . . . Catalogue* (New York, 1979), p. 588, no. 528. The names of Zenobius and Eustathius are given in Jerome, *Chronicle*, 233ff, under 336; by Theophanes, *Chronographia*, ed. C. de Boor (Leipzig, 1883) 1:33, under the year 5828 (=336); by Prosperus Aquitanus, *Chronicum integrum* (*PL*, 51:576), under the year 335–36. The Epiphanius basilica at Salamis on Cyprus (A. H. S. Megaw, "Byzantine Architecture and Decoration in Cyprus . . . ," *DOP* 28 [1974]:57ff, especially pp. 61f) of late fourth-century date shows the same plan, but it may as easily derive from Jerusalem as from Constantinople.

19 J. B. Ward-Perkins, in *The Great Palace of the Byzantine Emperors, Second Report*, ed. D. T. Rice (Edinburgh, 1959), p. 64, suggests that the rear wall of the propylaeum may be part of the fourth-century church. Th. Mathews, *Early Churches*, p. 19, expresses an opinion different from mine about the size and extent of the Constantinian cathedral.

20 For the Forum of Constantine, see Müller-Wiener, *Bildlexikon*, pp. 253ff. For its two-tiered colonnades, see Zosimus 2. 31. 1–3 (Paschoud, p. 104); Hesychios, *Patria* 41, in *Scriptores Originum Constantinopolitanarum*, ed. Th. Preger (Leipzig, 1901), p. 17; *Chronicon Paschale*, Ol. 277, 1(328) (*PG*, 92:708); Malalas 13. 321 (*PG*, 97:480).

For the Philadelphion and the tetrarchs, see Müller-Wiener, *Bildlexikon*, p. 267. For the porticoed streets of Constantinople, see ibid., p. 269. D. Claude, *Die byzantinische Stadt* (Munich, 1969), pp. 60ff, lists outstanding examples of late Roman porticoed streets, for instance at Gerasa (ibid., pp. 63).

21 On the column and its proposed reconstruction, see Müller-Wiener, *Bildlexikon*, pp. 255ff. C. Mango, "Constantinopolitana," *JDAI* 80 (1965):365ff, gives an interpretation of the socle relief, not quite convincing, in my opinion.

For the statue of Constantine, see: Dagron, *Constantinople*, pp. 40ff, 58; Philostorgios, *HE* 2. 17 (*PG*, 65:480; *GCS*, 21²:28); *Chronicon Paschale*, Ol. 277, 1 (328) (*PG*, 92:708ff), which says that the statue was brought from Phrygia; Malalas 13. 320 (*PG*, 97:480), who describes the statue as crowned with seven rays and specifies that it was brought from Ilion in Phrygia; Theophanes, *Chronographia*, 5970 (470), ed. C. de Boor, 2 vols. (Leipzig, 1883), 1:126; and Theophanes, *Chronographia*, 6034 (542), 1:222, who remarks the fall of the globe. For the illustration from the *Tabula Peutingeriana* and its date, see A. and M. Levi, *Itineraria Picta* (Rome, 1967), passim, especially pp. 169ff, and E. Weber, ed., *Tabula Peutingeriana* (Vienna, 1976), 1:segment VIII. 1.

22 For mansions in Antioch, see R. Stilwell, "Houses at Antioch," *DOP* 14 (1961):45ff. For mansions and ordinary housing in Constantinople, see: Chr. Strube, "Der Begriff domus in der Notitia urbis Constantinopolitanae," in Beck, *Studien*, pp. 121ff; A. Kriesis, "Über den Wohnhaustyp des frühen Konstantinopel," *BZ* 53 (1960):322ff. For suburbs beyond the walls, see V. Tiftixoglu, "Die Heleniani . . . ," in Beck, *Studien*, pp. 49ff. For zoning regulations, see Beck, *Studien*, pp. 10ff; some of these, dated 406–25, are outlined in *C Th* 15. 1. 45ff. The existence of high-rise buildings (Ph. Kukules, Βυζαντινῶν βίος καὶ πολιτίσμος, 3 vols. [Athens, 1951], 1:262ff) is doubted by Beck, *Studien*, p. 23, n. 39. Regarding church buildings in Constantinople attributed to Constantine, see his letter ordering bibles and expressing his expectations of a rapid increase in the Christian population (Eusebius, *VC* 3. 36 [Winkelmann, 100]). Jones, *Later Roman Empire*, p. 83, does not share my scepticism regarding Constantinian church building in Constantinople.

23 For the church of the Holy Apostles, see: A. Heisenberg, *Grabeskirche und Apostelkirche*, 2 vols. (Leipzig, 1908) 2:97 and 115ff.; A. Kaniuth, *Die Beisetzung Konstantins des Grossen*, Breslauer Historische Forschungen, 18 (Breslau, 1941); R. Krautheimer, "Zu Konstantins Apostelkirche in Konstantinopel," in Mullus, pp. 224ff; and idem, "A Note on Justinian's Church of the Holy Apostles . . . ," *Mélanges Eugène Tisserant*, vol. 2, *Studi e Testi* 232 (Vatican City, 1964), 2:265f (see also idem, *Studies*, pp. 27ff, 197ff). Müller-Wiener, *Bildlexikon*, pp. 465ff, has a fuller bibliography on the church of the Apostles and on the Fatih.

24 Eusebius, *VC* 4. 58–60 (Winkelmann, 144ff).

25 G. Prinzing and P. Speck, "Fünf Lokalitäten in Konstantinopel," in Beck, *Studien*, pp. 179ff, based on *Chronicon Paschale*, Ol. 281, 1 (*PG*, 92:721). Whether or not the imperial living quarters are identical with a "palace of Constantine" is discussed by Prinzing and Speck, "Fünf Lokalitäten," pp. 181ff.

26 Eusebius, *VC* 4. 60ff (Winkelmann, 145); Krautheimer, "Zu Konstantin's Apostelkirche." G. Downey, "The Builder of the Original Church of the Apostles," *DOP* 6 (1961):53ff, attributes the construction to Constantius, erroneously, in my opinion.

27 For the cross plan, see Gregory of Nazianz, Ἐνύπνιον περὶ τῆς Ἀναστασίας, v. 59ff (*PG*, 37:1258ff). For the church in Milan, see below, chapter 3 and notes 18ff. For those in Antioch and Gerasa, see: J. Lassus, "L'église cru-

ciforme," in *Antioch-on-the-Orontes*, Publications of the Committee for the Excavation of Antioch . . . , 2 (Princeton, N.J., 1938), pp. 5ff; J. Crowfoot, "The Christian Churches," in *Gerasa, City of the Decapolis*, ed. C. H. Kraeling (New Haven, 1938), pp. 26ff. For Eusebius's description of the church of the Apostles, see *VC* 4. 58 (Winkelmann, 144ff).

28 The οἶκος is mentioned in Socrates, *HE* 2. 38 (*PG*, 67:329ff); the "sacred στῆλαι," in Eusebius, *VC* 4. 60 (Winkelmann, 144ff).

29 The quotation is from Eusebius, *VC* 4. 71 (Winkelmann, 149ff). For the removal of the sarcophagus and the building of the mausoleum, see Krautheimer, "Zu Konstantins Apostelkirche," especially pp. 227ff.

30 For Constantinople as the πόλις ἐπώνυμος, see Eusebius, *VC* 4. 36 (Winkelmann, 133ff), quoting Constantine's rescript to Eusebius; see also ibid., 3. 48 (Winkelmann, 104ff), and Eusebius, *LC* 9 (Heikel, 221; *PG*, 20:1369ff). The quotation is from *C Th*, XIII, 5. 7 (December 1, 334).

31 For these neo-pagan comments, see Zosimus 2. 31 (Paschoud, 104).

32 Eusebius, *VC* 3. 54 (Winkelmann, 107ff).

33 C. Mango, "Antique Statuary"; Dagron, *Constantinople*, pp. 374ff.

34 For the statues of the Good Shepherd and Daniel in the lions' den, see Eusebius, *VC* 3. 49 (Winkelmann, 104ff); for the painting, see ibid., 3. 3 (Winkelmann, 82ff). The quotation regarding Christian shrines is from ibid., 3. 48 (Winkelmann, 104ff).

35 Dagron, *Constantinople*, pp. 367ff, especially 385ff. The Eusebius paraphrase is from *VC* 1. 43 (Winkelmann, 38ff). In 380 an epigram still addresses Theodosius I as the rising sun (*Anthologia Graeca* [XVI, 65] ed. H. Beckby, 4 vols., [Munich, 1965], 4:338). For this and the Christ-Helios link, see C. Davis-Weyer, "Das Traditio-Legis-Bild . . . ," *MJBK* 12 (1961):7ff, especially 24ff.

36 For the custom of bringing a statue of the emperor to the games, see Suetonius, *Vitae XII Caesarum* (Caesar, 76; Claudius, 11) (LCL, 1:98; 2:22).

37 Malalas 18. 484 (*PG*, 97:701ff).

38 The ritual at the column is described by Dagron, *Constantinople*, pp. 36ff. The quote from the late fourth century is in Philostorgius, *HE*, Epitome, 3. 17 (*PG*, 65:480; *GCS*, 21²:28): "Οὗτος ὁ θεόμαχος [this being Photius' designation of Philostorgius] καὶ τὴν Κωνσταντίνου εἰκόνα τὴν ἐπὶ του πορφυροῦ κίονος ἐσταμένην Θυσίαις τε ἰλάσκεσθαι, καῖ λυχνοκαΐαις καὶ Θυμιάμασι τιμᾶν καῖ εὐχὰς προσάγειν ὡς θεῷ καὶ ἀποτροπαίους ἱκετηρίας τῶν δεινῶν ἐπιτέλειν τοὺς χριστιανοὺς κατηγορεῖ. . . ." That from the fifth century is in

Theodoretos, *HE* 1. 32 (*PG*, 82:989): ". . . Εἰ δε τὶς . . . διαπίστει τὰ νῦν περὶ τὴν ἐκείνου Θήκην καὶ τὸν ἀνδρίαντα γενόμενα βλέπων πιστεύσατο τοῖς γεγραμμένοις. . . ." Those from 533 are in *Chronicon Paschale*, Ol. 328, 1 (*PG*, 92:889), and Malalas 18. 76 (*PG*, 97:693).

39 The quotation is from Theophanes, *Chronographia*, 5816 (307), 1:23. The reference to Malalas is *Chronographia*, 13 (*PG*, 97:480). The eighth-century text is Hesychios, *Patria* 2. 49 and 45a, in *Scriptores Originum Constantinopolitanarum*, ed. Preger, pp. 177f, 138.

40 For the tradition of Sol as the emperors' Divine Companion and its late disappearance from Constantine's coins, see chapter 1, note 15. For the inscription from Termessos, see K. Lańckoroński and G. Niemann, *Städte Pamphyliens und Pisidiens*, 2 vols. (Vienna, 1891), 1:206, n. 82.

41 Eusebius, *VC* 1. 34; 3. 10; 1. 2 (Winkelmann, 32f, 85f, and 15f).

42 F. J. Dölger, *Sol salutis* (Münster, 1925), *passim* (see especially pp. 66ff, on the Helios-Constantine statue); idem, "Das Sonnengleichnis einer Weihnachtspredigt . . . ," *Antike und Christentum* 6 (1940–50): 1ff; E. Kantorowicz, "Oriens Augusti-Lever du Roi," *DOP* 17 (1963):117ff, passim.

43 J. Toynbee and J. B. Ward-Perkins, *The Shrine of St. Peter* (London, 1956), pp. 71ff.

44 For the silver canopy placed by Constantine over Christ's tomb, see Eusebius, *VC* 3. 34 (Winkelmann, 99f) and representations on sixth-century ampullae— oil flasks bought as pilgrims' souvenirs (A. Grabar, *Les ampoules de Terre Sainte* [Paris, 1958]).

45 For Constantine's wanting to share the prayers addressed to the apostles, see Eusebius, *VC* 4. 60, 71 (Winkelmann, 144ff, 149ff), and Dörries, *Selbstzeugnis*, 413ff. For Constantine as their leader, see A. Kaniuth, *Die Beisetzung Konstantins des Grossen* (Breslau, 1941).

46 O. Weinreich, *Triskaidekadische Studien* (Giessen, 1916); idem., "Lykische Zwölfgötter-reliefs," *Sitzungsberichte der Heidelberger Akademie der Wissenschaften, Philosophisch-historische Klasse* (Heidelberg, 1913).

47 N. H. Baynes, *Constantine the Great and the Christian Church*, Proceedings of the British Academy, 15 (1929), pp. 1ff, esp. Appendix, pp. 95ff.

48 Heisenberg, *Grabeskirche und Apostelkirche*, 2:115, and J. Straub, "Konstantins christliches Sendungsbewusstsein," in *Regeneratio Imperii* (Darmstadt, 1972), pp. 70ff.

49 P. Franchi de' Cavalieri, "I funerali ed il sepolcro di Costantino Magno," *MEFR* 36 (1916–17):205ff.

50 J. Straub, "Constantine as κὸινος επίσκοπος," *DOP* 21 (1967):37ff.

51 *ILCV*, p. 1752.

52 N. H. Baynes, "Eusebius and the Christian Empire," in *Byzantine Studies and Other Essays* (London, 1955), pp. 168ff (first published 1933–34); E. Peterson, "Der Monotheismus als politisches Problem," *Theologische Traktate* (Munich, 1951), pp. 55ff (first published 1935); G. Ladner, *The Idea of Reform* (Cambridge, Mass., 1959), pp. 117ff.

53 Ladner, *The Idea of Reform*, p. 121.

54 Eusebius, *VC* 4. 73 (Winkelmann, 150), P. Bruun, "The Consecration Coins of Constantine the Great," *Arctos*, n.s. 1 (1954), pp. 19ff, and L. Koep, "Die Konsekrationsmünzen Konstantins . . . ," *JAC* 1 (1958):94ff, both have traced the roots of the type in older Roman coinage and have interpreted the Constantinian variant and its political and religious implications. With regard to the latter, it is interesting to note the resemblance between Constantine's christianized *consecratio* and the Ascension of Christ on the well-known ivory in Munich (W. F. Volbach, *Elfenbeinarbeiten der Spätantike und des frühen Mittelalters*, 3rd ed. [Mainz, 1916], p. 53, no. 56), where Christ is shown grasping the hand of God as he strides heavenward. David Wright was good enough to call the coin to my attention and to provide me with a splendid photograph of a sample at the Bibliothèque Nationale in Paris.

55 See the revival of the *consecratio* scene in the British Museum ivory claimed for the late fourth century by J. Straub, "Die Himmelfahrt des Julianus Apostata," *Gymnasium* 69 (1962):310ff, convincing to me, notwithstanding the fifth-century date proposed by K. Wessel, "Eine Gruppe oberitalischer Elfenbeinarbeiten," *JDAI* 63-64 (1950):143ff, and others.

56 2 Kings 2:11.

57 *Reallexikon für Antike und Christentum*, ed. Th. Klauser, (Stuttgart, 1959), 4:1153ff, s.v. "Elias, Himmelfahrt," and 1157ff, s.v. "Frühchristliche Kunst" (K. Wessel).

III. Milan

1 *Storia di Milano*, 1, provides a reliable survey of the history (pp. 244ff) and of the archaeology (pp. 493ff) of Roman Milan. On the latter, see also the fascicles of the Forma Urbis Mediolani, ed. A. de Capitani d'Arzago, A. Calderini, and others (Milan, 1937–43).

2 On the amphitheater, see A. Calderini, *L'Anfiteatro Romano*, Forma Urbis Mediolani, 2 (Milan, 1938); M. Mirabella Roberti, "Quattro edifici di éta tardoantica . . . ," *Arte Lombarda* 15 (1970):111ff; on the circus, A. de Capitani

d'Arzago, *Il Circo Romano*, Forma Urbis Mediolani, 1 (1937), and *Storia di Milano*, 1, pp. 530ff; on the presumable location of the palace, ibid., pp. 548ff; on the colonnades and the tetrapylon in Via Romana, A. de Capitani d'Arzago, *La zona di Porta Romana*, Forma Urbis Mediolani, 5 (1943), and *Storia di Milano*, 1, pp. 558ff.

3 The archaeological evidence on the mausoleum as presented in A. Pica and P. Portalupo, *La Basilica Porziana di S. Vittore al Corpo* (Milan, 1934), is superseded by M. Mirabella Roberti, "Il recinto fortificato Romano di San Vittore a Milano," *Castellum* 6 (1967):95ff. The written sources on its plan and decoration are excerpted in U. Monneret de Villard, "Note di archeologia Lombarda," *Arch St Lomb* 41 (1914):5ff, especially 12ff. The *veduta*, together with others done by the same draughtsman in Milan and Rome, all in the Graphische Sammlung, Staatsgalerie, Stuttgart, was first published, but not identified, by C. von Fabriczy, "Il libro di schizzi di un pittore olandese," *Archivio Storico dell'Arte* 6 (1893):106ff, especially 118ff; it was recognized as a view of S. Vittore by P. Arrigoni, "Una veduta milanese cinquecentesca identificata," *Arch St Lomb* 54 (1927):358ff. On the sixteenth-century rebuilding of the church, see W. Lotz, in L. H. Heydenreich and W. Lotz, *Architecture in Italy, 1400–1600, The Pelican History of Art* (Harmondsworth, 1974), pp. 294ff and passim. On the porphyry sarcophagus, possibly Maximian's, see Ambrose's letter to Theodosius, Epp. 1. 53 (*PL*, 16:1215ff), regarding the transfer to Milan of the body of Valentinian II, "est ibi porphyreticum labrum pulcherimum . . . nam et Maximianus . . . ita humatus est . . . ," and Alciati's report, as quoted by Monneret de Villard, "Note di archeologia Lombarda," but doubted by recent writers (see Kinney, 1970–71, p. 32, n. 103).

4 The quotations are from the *Ordo urbium nobilium* of Ausonius (*LCL*, 1:272):

> Et Mediolani mira omnia, copia rerum
> innumerae cultaeque domus, facunda virorum
> ingenia et mores laeti; tum duplice muro
> amplificata loci species populique voluptas
> circus et inclusi moles cuneata theatri;
> templa Palatinaeque arces opulensque moneta
> et regio Herculei celebris sub honore lavacri;
> cunctaque marmoreis ornata peristylia signos
> moeniaque in valli formam circumdata limbo:
> excellent: nec iuncta premit vicinia Romae.

The *terminus post* for the composition of the little work is provided by its reference to the defeat at Aquileia in 383 of the usurper Maximus (*LCL*, 1:274).

For the population estimate, uncertain at that, see *Storia di Milano*, 1, pp. 286ff.

5 The following survey of the struggles between Nicenes and anti-Nicenes, condensed as it is by necessity, oversimplifies and thus distorts the complexity of the issues, the shading in position among the leaders on either side, and the shifts that occurred as the contest dragged on over half a century. To inform myself on

a subject so far removed from my own field, I have used what seem to me two well-balanced presentations: extensively, Lïetzmann, passim; and concisely, H. Chadwick, *The Early Church, Pelican History of the Church* (Harmonds-worth, 1975), pp. 133ff. I have also looked, though not much more than that, into the most important sources, such as Athanasius, *Apologia ad Constantium* and *Historia Arianorum* (*PG*, 25:595ff, 695ff).

6 On the synod of Milan and subsequent events, see: Jerome, *Chronicle*, 239ff, under the year 355; Rufinus, *Historia Ecclesiastica* 1. 20 (*PL*, 21:493ff); Lucifer of Cagliari, *Pro Dei filio moriendum* (CSEL, 14:284ff). See also Lietzmann, 3:215ff, and *Storia di Milano*, 1, pp. 312ff. On Liberius's opposition and subsequent recantation, see: *LP*, 1, introduction, cxxi; Jerome, *Chronicle*, under the year 349, 237ff; and Lietzmann, 3:224ff.

7 On Auxentius, see *Lexikon für Theologie und Kirche*, 8 vols. (Freiburg, Br., 1957), 1:1138ff; his lack of Latin is intimated by Athanasius, *Historia Arianorum*, 75 (*PG*, 25:784ff). The general situation under his episcopate in Milan is summed up by M. Simonetti, "La politica antiariana di Ambrogio," in *Ambrosius Episcopus, Atti del Congresso Internazionale di Studi Ambrosiani . . . , 1974* (Milan, 1976), pp. 266ff. On Valentinian's policy, see Lietzmann, 4:16ff, and Jones, *Later Roman Empire*, pp. 150ff and 1098, n. 33, referring to Ammianus Marcellinus, *Rerum gestarum libri XXX* 9. 5 (LCL, 3:370ff), and Sozomenos, *HE* 6. 7 (*PG*, 67:1312ff), the latter reporting the quotation given in our text.

8 On Ambrose's election, see Paulinus, *Vita sancti Ambrosii*, 6ff (*PL*, 14:30ff). On his baptism, see ibid., and Jerome, *Chronicle*, 217ff, under the year 374. As to the day, it was December 7 or 8; since the latter was a Sunday, it seems preferable. On the background of the election, presumably influenced by the government, see Simonetti, "La politica antiariana," and C. Corbellini, "Sesto Petronio Probo e l'elezione episcopale di Ambrogio," *Rendiconti Istituto Lombardo di Scienze e Lettere* 109 (1975): 181ff, as quoted by M. Sordi, "Ambrogio di fronte a Roma e al paganesimo," in *Ambrosius Episcopus*, ed. G. Lazzari, 2 vols. (Milan, 1976), 1:203ff. On his consistent policy, both anti-Arian and opposed to temporal interference, see ibid., Simonetti, "La politica antiariana," and Lietzmann, 4:58ff; see also the concise summary given by S. Lewis, "The Latin Iconography of the Single-Naved Cruciform Basilica Apostolorum," *Art Bulletin* 51 (1969):205ff. For the clash with Theodosius, see Lietzmann, 4:88ff, based on Ambrosius, *De obitu Theodosii*, 34 (CSEL, 73:388ff), and Theodoret, *HE* 5. 17 (or 18) (*PG*, 82:1232ff).

9 *C Th*, XVI, 5. 5 (August 3, 379), revokes an earlier tolerance decree issued at Sirmium in August or September of the preceding year. See also: Socrates, *HE* 5. 1 (*PG*, 67:568ff); Sozomenos, *HE* 7.1 (ibid., 1417ff), Ambrose, *De Fide*, 1, prol. 1 (CSEL, 78:3ff); and idem., Epp. 1. 1 (*PL*, 16:914ff), preceded by Gratian's request for instruction (ibid., 913ff). For the events in 386, see below, pp. 88–89.

10 For recent surveys of fourth- and fifth-century church building in Milan, see: *Storia di Milano*, 1, pp. 591ff; G. Traversari, *Architettura paleocristiana Milanese* (Milan, 1964); Krautheimer, *Pelican³*, pp. 82ff. The written sources have been compiled and interpreted, if at times erroneously, by A. Calderini, "La tradizione letteraria più antica sulle basiliche milanesi," *Rendiconti Istituto Lombardo* 75 (1941–42): 69ff.

11 On the cathedral, see M. Mirabella Roberti, "La cattedrale antica di Milano e il suo battistero," *Arte Lombarda* 8 (1963): 77ff, and idem, "Topografia e architettura anteriori al Duomo," in *Atti del Congresso Internazionale sul Duomo di Milano*, 2 vols. (Milan, 1969), 1:31ff. Both studies complete and in part supersede the report on the first excavation, A. de Capitani d'Arzago, *La chiesa maggiore di Milano* (Milan, 1952). On the irregularities of the plan and their possible link to the street system, see: de Capitani d'Arzago, *La chiesa maggiore*, pp. 110ff; Mirabella Roberti, "La cattedrale antica," pp. 81ff; and idem, "Topografia e architettura anteriori al Duomo," esp. p. 40, n. 3.

12 On the existence in 386 of both the new and the old cathedrals, see Ambrose, Epp. 1. 20. 10ff and 24ff (*PL*, 16: 1039ff and 1044ff). Suggestions that the *vetus* was located outside the town and was identical with S. Vittore al Corpo (e.g., A. de Capitano d'Arzago, "L'architettura cristiana a Milano," *II, CEB . . . Paris . . . 1948*, [Paris 1951], 2: 67ff) can safely be eliminated. On the baptistery found below the Duomo, see "Relazione dell'Ufficio regionale," *Arch St Lomb* 26 (1899): 170ff, and E. Cattaneo, "Appunti sui battisteri antichi di Milano," *Instituto Lombardo, Rendiconti Letterari* 103 (1969): 849ff, especially 859.

13 Socrates, *HE* 2. 36 (*PG* 67: 300ff), on the size of the synod of 355. For the construction of the new cathedral, Mirabella Roberti, "Topografia e architettura anteriori al Duomo," pp. 33ff, proposes a date in the first half of the fourth century, whether under Mirocles, already bishop in 313, or under Dionysius, around 350. The remark on Constans's generosity is contained in Athanasius, *Apologia ad Constantium*, 7 (*PG*, 25: 604ff): ". . . ὅτι ὁ μὲν μακαρίτης ἀδέλφος τοὺ τὰς ἐκκλησίας ἀναθημάτων ἐπλήρωσεν." Needless to say, ἐκκλησίας in this context means congregations, not church buildings.

14 Mirabella Roberti, "La cattedrale antica" and "Topografia e architettura anteriori al Duomo," in conformity with previous consensus; for my own opinion, see below, note 33.

15 W. Kleinbauer, "Toward a dating of San Lorenzo in Milan," *Arte Lombarda* 13 (1968): 1ff, and S. Rufolo, "Le strutture murarie degli edifici paleocristiani milanesi," *Rivista dell'Istituto Nazionale di Archeologia e Storia dell'Arte*, n.s. 17 (1970, published 1972): 5ff, have interpreted the changing masonry technique of Milanese fourth-century buildings as a gauge for the chronological development of local church architecture. However, Lewis, 1973, pp. 201ff, has already pointed convincingly to the impact of strong financial backing or its lack on the quality of workmanship in construction. Regarding Ambrose's fi-

nancial limitations, see the remark in his *De excessu fratris* 1. 20 (CSEL, 73:220ff): "tu . . . in quo domestica sollecitudo testor animam tuam me in fabricis ecclesiae id saepe veritum esse, ne displicerem tibi . . . ; denique obiurgaste moram . . . ," suggesting a need to go slowly on the building of churches so as to keep within the family budget.

16 E. Dassmann, "Ambrosius und die Märtyrer," *JAC* 18 (1975):49ff; Lewis, 1969, pp. 93ff; see also P. Brown, *The Cult of the Saints* (Chicago, 1980), pp. 36f.

17 On the fourth-century church, see G. Landriani, *La basilica ambrosiana* (Milan, 1889); M. Mirabella Roberti, "Contributi della ricerca archeologica all'architettura ambrosiana Milanese," in *Ambrosius Episopus*, 1:335ff. See Krautheimer, *Pelican*[3], pp. 185f and note for bibliography. On the burials below the altar, see Ambrose, Epp. 1. 21. 1ff and 13 (*PL*, 16:1062ff, 1066ff); see also Dassmann, "Ambrosius," pp. 52ff, and Brown, *Cult of the Saints*, pp. 36f, both stressing Ambrose's aim to incorporate "the veneration of the martyrs into the sacramental-liturgical life of the congregation." My own feeling is that the enthusiasm of his flock forced Ambrose to search for relics.

18 The fourth-century church was first traced by Don Enrico Villa, "La basilica ambrosiana degli Apostoli . . . ," *Ambrosius* 39, suppl. 2 (1963):15ff, with reference to his preliminary publications. It has also been discussed by: Lewis, 1969, pp. 83ff; idem, *Art Bulletin* 51 (1960):205ff; F. Tolotti, "Le absidi di S. Silvestro a Roma e di San Nazaro a Milano," *MEFRA* 85 (1973):713ff.

19 R. Delbrueck, "Das Silberreliquiar von S. Nazaro in Mailand," *Antike Denkmaler*, 4, fasc. 1 (Berlin, 1927), pp. 1ff. For a comparable reliquary casket, in all likelihood Constantinopolitan, see M. Panayotidi and A. Grabar, "Un Reliquaire paléochrétien découvert près de Théssalonique," *CA* 24 (1975):33ff. On the debated original termination of the east arm of the Milanese Apostoleion, see Villa, "La basilica ambrosiana," passim, and Mirabella Roberti, "Contributi della ricerca archeologica," as against Lewis, 1969, pp. 89ff, and Tolotti, "Le absidi," pp. 747ff.

20 Krautheimer, "Zu Konstantins Apostelkirche in Konstantinopel," in *Mullus*, pp. 224ff.

21 It is tempting to see a further analogy between Ambrose's Apostle church and its Constantinopolitan model: just as in Constantinople Constantine's mausoleum was placed by Constantius in the late fifties against the façade of his father's Apostoleion, so in Milan the Trivulzio Chapel is attached to the façade of Ambrose's church. Indeed, thirty years ago Don Villa, as I see from my notes, mentioned to me the existence of Early Christian walls underneath the Trivulzio Chapel, and F. Tolotti, "Tre basiliche paleocristiane," in *Miscellanea Giulio Belvederi* (Vatican City, 1954), pp. 369ff, especially p. 376, suggested its having taken the place of a fourth-century chapel. See also Lewis, 1969, p. 90 n. 18, and idem, "Problems of Architectural Style and the Ambrosian Liturgy in Late

Fourth-Century Milan," in *Hortus imaginum*, ed. R. Enggass and M. Stokstad (Lawrence, Kans., 1974), pp. 11ff, especially pp. 16ff. I, for one, prefer to leave the question open.

22 Two fragments of Ambrose's dedicatory inscription (*ILCV*, 1800) were found in the 1950s (Villa, "La basilica ambrosiana," pp. 32f):

> condidit ambrOSIUS templum dominoque sacravit
> nomine AposTOLico munere reliquiis
> forma crucis tEMPlum est templum victoria Christi
> sacra triumphalis signat imago locum
> in capite est templi vitae Nazarius almae
> et sublime solum martyris exuviis
> crux ubi sacratum caput extulit orbe reflexo
> hoc caput est templo Nazarioque domus
> qui fovet aeternam victor pietate quietem
> crux cui palma fuit crux etiam sinus est

23 For the Milanese relics, see the *Martyrologium Hieronymianum*, AASS, Nov. II. 2, 241, under May 9: "Mediolano de ingressu reliquiarum apostolorum Johannis, Andreae et Thomae in basilicam ad portam Romanam." See also H. Delehaye, *Les origines du culte des martyrs*,[2] (Brussels, 1933), pp. 338ff.

The story accepted over and over again—that the relics were brought from Rome by Simplicianus, then one of Ambrose's presbyters—with its implication that they were of Peter and Paul, appears to go back to Landulf the Elder's *Mediolanensis Historia* 1. 6 (*RIS*, 4:63ff, quoted in A. Porter, *Lombard Architecture*, 3 vols. [New Haven, 1916], 2:633ff), and thus would not antedate the late eleventh century. To me it seems untrustworthy.

For the transfer to Constantinople of the remains of Timothy, Andrew, and Luke, see: Jerome, *Chronicle*, 240ff, ad an. 356 and 357; Philostorgios, *HE* 3. 2 (*PG*, 65:480ff); and *Chronicon Paschale*, ad an. 356 and 357 (*PG*, 92:783ff). Relics of the garments of John the Evangelist, Andrew, and Thomas entered the church only in the tenth century (Janin, *Eglises*, pp. 50ff).

For the entry under November 27, "in Mediolano Lucae Andreae, Johannis . . . et Eufemiae," see *Martyrologium Hieronymianum*, AASS, Nov. II. 2, 623ff. For that under September 3, "in Aquileia dedicatio basilicae et ingressio reliquiarum sanctorum Andreae Apostoli Lucae Johannis Eufemiae," see ibid., 485ff. See also Delehaye, *Les origines*, pp. 332ff, 338ff.

24 E. Arslan, "Osservazioni preliminari sulla basilica . . . di S. Simpliciano . . . ," *Arch St Lomb*, n.s. 10 (1947), pp. 5ff; idem, "Qualche dato sulla basilica . . . di San Simpliciano," *RAC* 23–24 (1947–48):367ff; idem, "Nuovi ritrovamenti in S. Simpliciano . . . ," *Bollettino d'Arte* 43 (1958):199ff; idem, "Ultime novità a San Simpliciano," *Arte Lombarda* 6 (1961):149ff; M. Mirabella Roberti, "Milano—Basilica di S. Simpliciano," in *Studi e Ricerche nel Territorio della Provincia di Milano* (Milan, 1967), pp. 166ff.

25 Suffice it to list for S. Lorenzo only the most important bibliography of recent date: P. Verzone, *L'Architettura religiosa dell'Alto Medioevo nell'Italia set-*

tentrionale (Milan, 1942), pp. 79ff, proposing a mid-fifth-century date. Present research, however, though diverging on the exact date, agrees on the fourth century: see CCC, passim; W. E. Kleinbauer, "Some Renaissance Views of San Lorenzo in Milan," *Arte Lombarda* 12 (1967): 1ff; idem, "Toward a dating of San Lorenzo . . . ," *Arte Lombarda* 13 (1968): 1ff; idem, "Edita in turribus . . . ," *Gesta* 15 (1976): 1ff; Kinney, 1970–71, pp. 13ff; idem, 1972, pp. 92ff; Lewis, 1973, pp. 197ff.

26 The first reference to S. Lorenzo by name occurs in Gregory of Tours, *Liber in gloria martyrum* (*MGH SS rer. Mer.*, 1 : 518ff). For the chapel of S. Sisto there is an epigram, "in basilicam sancti Syxti . . . quam Laurentius episcopus fecit," composed by Ennodius, *Magni Felicis Ennodii opera* (CSEL, 6 : 559ff), and dedicated to Bishop Lawrence (493 – 511). Likewise, Bishop Lawrence may have dedicated to Saint Hippolyt the chapel of S. Ippolito. S. Aquilino first appears under that name in the fifteenth century, and its former dedication to S. Genesius cannot be traced back beyond the early fourteenth century.

27 On the platform, see CCC, passim and summary, pp. 81ff; Kinney, 1970–71, pp. 17ff and n. 22; idem, 1972, pp. 98ff.

28 CCC, p. 87, as an alternative to a reconstruction with columns, suggest that the Romanesque octagonal piers which at present support the exedrae on the ground floor were cut from original square supports, remains of which they see in the square plinths which are monolithic with the eight-sided bottom blocks. I would conjecturally interpret, instead, the plinths as the residues of pedestals, nearly as high as wide—that is, roughly one meter wide and carrying columns ca. five meters high, including bases and shafts. The proportions would correspond to those of the colonnade in the Anastasis Rotunda in Jerusalem. On the vaulting of the galleries, see CCC, pp. 133ff. For the vault of the center square, CCC, loc. cit., have proposed a groin vault, while Verzone, *L'Architettura religiosa*, pp. 82ff, remained undecided whether to prefer this or a dome. Kleinbauer, "Edita in turribus," pp. 1ff and n. 4, favors a groin vault, withdrawing his earlier tentative proposals ("Some Renaissance Views," pp. 1ff) for a reconstruction with either a dome or a pyramidal timber roof. Lewis, 1973, pp. 214ff, decides in favor of the latter, claiming erroneously, "the virtual impossibility that the tetraconch itself was vaulted."

29 For the elevation of S. Lorenzo, both interior and exterior, as rebuilt after the fire of 1071 (and possibly with later medieval repairs), see the survey drawing preserved at the Castello Sforzesco (Raccolta Bianconi, 4, our fig. 77) among the projects for the sixteenth-century remodeling. The survey presumably dates from that campaign: the diagonal cross corner walls are in bare masonry (or could they date from a late medieval repair?). For the sixteenth-century rebuilding, see Lotz, in *Architecture in Italy*, pp. 299ff.

The quotation is from the eighth-century *Laudes Mediolani civitatis* (*Monumenta Germaniae Historica, Poetae Latini aevi carolingi*, 1 : 25). The emendation of the unintelligible *alavariis* into *aula variis* is due to a suggestion of D. Kinney. For a description of the church about 1070, see *Benzonis episcopi*

Albensis ad Henricum IV . . . (*MGH SS*, 11:680): "aula tam mirabilis // porphyreticis exstructa cum aureis laminis"—hence presumably gold foil. For a few years later, see *Arnulfi gesta episcoporum Mediolanensium* (*MGH SS*, 8:24ff), lamenting the fire, "quae fuerunt lignorum lapidumque sculpturae eorumque altrinsecus compaginatae iuncturae quae suis columpnae cum basibus, tribunalem quoque per gyrum ac desuper tegens universa musyvum. . . ." For the reconstruction of the exterior, see Kleinbauer, "Edita in turribus."

30 On the narthex, its ground floor at either end terminated by apses, and on the atrium, see M. Mirabella Roberti, "Una nota sul nartece di San Lorenzo," in *Studi in onore di Mons. Carlo Castiglioni* (Milan, 1957), pp. 473ff, and J.-Ch. Picard, "Topografia urbana e vita cittadina nell'Alto Medioevo," *MEFRA* 85 (1973):691ff.

31 See Krautheimer, *Pelican*³, pp. 79ff, on the Golden Octagon and on the origins and function of the genus, with reference to previous bibliography. See also idem, "Success and Failure in Late Antique Church Building," in *Age of Spirituality*, ed. K. Weitzmann (New York, 1980), pp. 121ff. For H. Sophia, see chapter 2, note 17.

32 On the architecture and the surviving decoration of S. Aquilino, see CCC, pp. 106ff and passim, and, summarily, Kinney, 1970–71, pp. 13ff; on the mosaics, see CCC, pp. 201ff; on its function as a mausoleum rather than a baptistery, see Kinney, 1970–71, pp. 19ff, and Lewis, 1973, pp. 220ff. For the lost interior decoration, see the sources quoted in Kinney, 1970–71, n. 10.

33 Kinney, 1972, passim. Lewis, 1973, argues for the start of construction at S. Lorenzo between 389 and 391 with the financial backing of Theodosius and for its completion prior to 402. On the date of the demolition of the amphitheater prior to the composition of Ausonius' *Ordo urbium nobilium*, see Kinney, 1972, pp. 99ff.

   Regarding the "luxury character" of the masonry of S. Lorenzo as against that of Ambrose's churches, see Lewis, 1973, pp. 201ff. It is precisely the high-quality building technique and the *opus sectile* revetment (M. Mirabella Roberti, "Topografia e architettura anteriori al Duomo," pp. 33ff; Ruffolo, "Le strutture murarie") which make me wonder whether the baptistery did perhaps enjoy financial support greater than could be provided by Ambrose and, hence, whether it was built at the same time as the cathedral or not much later, when imperial subsidies were still flowing. Ambrose then would have only composed the epigram for the interior of the baptistery.

34 Kinney, 1972. See, however, Lewis, 1973, who falls back on the traditional thesis of S. Aquilino's construction by Galla Placidia for her mausoleum.

35 The argument is the subject of Ambrose's famous letter, Epp. 1. 20 (*PL*, 16:1036ff; see also the summary provided by Calderini, "La tradizione letteraria," pp. 71ff). The identification of the Basilica Portiana with S. Lorenzo,

first proposed with strong reasons by A. de Capitani d'Arzago, *La chiesa maggiore*, pp. 18ff, and CCC, pp. 181ff and 246ff, is upheld on further grounds by Kinney, 1972, pp. 103ff. Older identifications—with S. Vittore al Corpo (Pica and Portalupi, *La Basilica Porziana*, passim) or with S. Eustorgio (I. Schuster, *S. Ambrogio e le più antiche basiliche milanesi* [Milan, 1940], pp. 56ff; known to me only through A. Calderini, "Le basiliche dell'età ambrosiana in Milano," in *Ambrosiana* [Milan, 1942], pp. 137ff, especially pp. 144ff)—are as unconvincing to me as the recently proposed equations of the Portiana with a basilica attached to the circus and excavated in the sixties (M. Mirabella Roberti, as quoted by M. Cagiano de Azevedo," Lo hortus Philippi di Mediolanum," *IX CAC* . . . *1975*, 2 vols. [Vatican City, 1978], 2:133ff; but see its earlier interpretation as a consistorium, intimated by M. Mirabella Roberti, *VIII CAC* . . . *Barcelona* . . . *1969*, p. 131, n. 13) or with "a small and probably ancient titulus church outside the walls" (Lewis, 1973, pp. 203ff). The quotations are from Ambrose, Epp. 1. 20. 1ff (*PL*, 16:1036ff), and ibid., 19ff (*PL*, 16:1042). On preparing the emperor's pew, see ibid., 4 (*PL* 16:1037): "nuntiatum est mihi . . . quod ad Portianam basilicam de palatio decanos misissent et vela suspenderent . . ."; also ibid., 20: "cortinas regias esse collectas. . . ." For the correct interpretation of the *decani* as janitors or messengers and the *vela* or *cortinae* as curtains to segregate the emperor's pew, see *PW*, 4:2246, and 7:2219.

36 Ambrose, *De spiritu sancto* 1. 1. 19ff (CSEL, 79:24ff), written before Easter 381 and based on sermons delivered in 380 (ibid., introduction, 17*):

> super omnia spiritus sanctus est . . . expressius non morabor . . . cum ita te adsertione istiusmodi testificatus sis proxime delectatum, ut basilicam ecclesiae sine ullo monitore praeceperis reformari. . . .Neque enim aliud possumus dicere nisi quod ignorantibus omnibus subito basilicam reddidisti. Spiritus . . . sancti hoc opus est qui a nobis tunc praedicabatur. . . . Nec superioris temporis damna deploro. . . . Etenim basilicam sequestrasti ut fidem probares. Implevit igitur propositum suum pietas tua, quae sic sequestraverat, ut probaret, sic probavit ut redderet. . . .

For an excellent analysis of the situation, see Kinney, 1972, pp. 103ff and n. 78. I incline to deviate from it only in that I think the sequester was ordered, not so much on behalf of the anti-Nicenes, as to secure the church during arbitration: "basilicam sequestrasti ut fidem probares . . ."; that is, Gratian was undecided, but was convinced by Ambrose's insistent catechizing on the problem of Christ's consubstantiality.

On the disputation with the two chamberlains, see Paulinus, *Vita Sancti Ambrosii* 18 (*PL* 14:35ff).

37 On the events of 385, see Ambrose, Epp. 1. 29, *Sermo contra Auxentium de basilicis tradendis* (*PL* 16:1058ff): "Superiore anno quando ad palatium sum petitus . . . cum imperator basilicam vellet eripere . . . quando comiti militari cum expeditis ad fugandam multitudinem egresso obtulerunt omnes se neci pro fide Christi . . ."; for the new tolerance decree, see *C Th*, XVI, 1. 4, addressed January 23, 386, to the *praefectus praetorio*; for the decrees of 378 and 379, see above, note 9, and below, note 39.

On Justina, see *PW*, 10:1338ff (Seeck); see also Socrates, *HE* 5. 11. 4 (*PG*, 67:595ff), and Sozomenos, *HE* 7. 13 (*PG*, 67:1147ff).

38 For a dating in the episcopate of Auxentius, see Krautheimer, *Pelican*², p. 82 (but revoked in the third edition, pp. 82ff); Kinney, 1972, pp. 103ff. For the bishop's, whether "Arian" or Nicene, having officiated at S. Tecla, see Kinney, 1972, loc. cit., and Lewis 1973, pp. 204ff. For the identification of S. Lorenzo as the palace church, here revoked, see Krautheimer, *Pelican*, loc. cit., and Kinney, 1972, pp. 101ff.

39 The vacillating policy of Gratian at the time is reflected in a series of decrees: *C Th*, XVI, 5, dated August 3, 379, from Milan revokes a previous tolerance decree of unknown date issued at Sirmium. The latter, however, was preceded by one of orthodox character, *C Th*, XVI, 5. 4, issued April 22, 376 or 378. *C Th*, XVI, 5. 6 and 5. 7 (January 10 and May 8, 381), again outline an energetically Catholic policy. On Flavia Maxima Constantia, see *PW*, 4:959, and Ambrose, *De spiritu sancto* (CSEL, 79:317ff, index), where she is designated *ariana*; on Gratian's character, see *Epitome de Caesaribus*, in Sextus Aurelius Victor, *Liber de Caesaribus* (ed. F. Pichlmayr, rev. R. Gruendel [Leipzig, 1970], pp. 173ff).

40 On the burial of Valentinian I at Constantinople, see Ammianus Marcellinus, *Rerum gestarum libri* 30. 10. 1 (LCL, 3:372ff), and Ph. Grierson, "The Tombs and Obits of the Byzantine Emperors," *DOP* 16 (1962):1ff, especially 42ff. On the tombs of Gratian and Valentinian II, apparently close together, see Ambrose, *De Obitu Valentiniani* 79 (CSEL, 73:366): "Gratiane et Valentiniane . . . quam sepulcra vicina. . . ." I am not so sure that the *communis opinio* is right in assuming that their bodies were ever brought to Milan from Vienne, where both brothers died; the passage *De obitu Valentiniani* 28 (ibid., 343ff), "ego tuus [Valentinian's] legatus repetivi Gallias . . . qua fraternas reliquias postulabas," does not suggest the success of Ambrose's mission, nor does Epp. 1. 53 (*PL*, 16:1215ff), containing Ambrose's report to Theodosius on the availability at Milan of a porphyry sarcophagus and/or porphyry slabs for Valentinian's burial ("est hic porphyreticum labrum . . . sunt tabulae porphyreticae pretiosissimae quibus vestiatur opusculum quo regales exuviae claudantur. . . .") and acknowledging the receipt of Theodosius's permission to that end ("Et ipsius igitur consuletur et charissimis exuviis si acceleretur sepultura ne aestivo penitus solvantur calore. . . ."), prove that the burial ever took place. Ambrose seems to have expected final orders ("exspectabatur rescriptum clementiae tuae . . ."), and the outbreak of Eugenius's revolt on August 22 may have intervened. But even assuming the burial of Valentinian II had taken place at Milan as envisaged, no mention is made of Gratian, and nothing suggests that either brother or both was buried at S. Vittore al Corpo, as Kinney, 1970–71, pp. 33ff.

On Flavia Maxima Constantia's body being brought to Constantinople, see *PW*, 4:959; on Justina's reconciliation with Ambrose (and Nicene orthodoxy?), see Socrates, *HE* 11 (*PG*, 67:595).

Kinney's tentative proposal (idem, 1970–71, pp. 31ff) to the effect that

Justina was buried in the "Capella Reginae," S. Aquilino, seems to me plausible, presuming that she died (in 388) reconciled with Nicene orthodoxy. I only disagree with the suggestion (ibid., loc. cit.) that she could have built it for herself—prior to 378, after all—she moved to Milan only in the autumn of that year.

41 LP, 1:207; Socrates, HE 5. 7, with reference to Matthew 10:23 (PG, 67:576).

42 Ambrose, De fide ad Gratianum Augustum (CSEL, 78:3ff).
      The date of the composition of De fide, proposed in the preface (CSEL, 8* and 10*), is September 378 for books 1 and 2, the end of 380 for books 3 to 5. The former date is based on the passage, ibid., 2, "solus Augustus totius orbis," hence after the death of Valens, August 9, 378, and before the cooption of Theodosius, January 19, 379. The phrase, ibid., 3ff, "ad proelium profecturus," in this case cannot refer (as Lietzmann, 4:607) to Gratian's coming to Valens's aid in July 378. The passage must refer to a campaign envisaged in the fall of 378, perhaps against the Goths after the defeat of Valens. Nor can Gratian and Ambrose have met in July 378. Gratian at that time was rushing down the Danube from Germany to Sirmium to assist Valens (Ammianus Marcellinus, Rerum gestarum libri 31. 11. 6), and Ambrose, from what is known, did not leave Milan. They seem to have met first in March 379, when Gratian returned from Sirmium to Trier (Jones, Later Roman Empire, pp. 163ff).

43 On Auxentius II–Mercurinus, see PW, 15:974 (Ensslin). Dale Kinney points out both that his appointment would have escalated the conflict and that during Easter week, when baptism was performed, by the bishop only, both Nicenes and "Arians" were more than ever in need of a cathedral of their own.

44 Lewis, 1973, pp. 211ff, sees in S. Ippolito a martyrium chapel dedicated to Saint Lawrence. On S. Lorenzo's serving as the Milanese bishops' mausoleum, see Verzone, L'Architettura religiosa, pp. 88ff; see also Lewis, 1973, p. 212, n. 71, quoting a later publication of Verzone's which is unknown to me.

IV. Rome Again

1 On the layout of Constantinian Rome and the monuments on the Forum, see above, chapter 1 and note 1. On the "loggia" near the Forum Boarium, see G. B. Giovenale, La Basilica di S. Maria in Cosmedin (Rome, 1927), pp. 334ff.

2 On the pagan resistance and revival, see A. Alföldi, A Conflict of Ideas in the Late Fourth Century (Oxford, 1952); A. Momigliano, ed., The Conflict between Paganism and Christianity, Oxford-Warburg Studies (Oxford, 1963); Peter Brown, Augustine of Hippo (Berkeley and Los Angeles, 1967); Convegno . . . tardo antico e alto Medioevo, Accademia Nazionale dei Lincei, quaderno 105 (Rome, 1968), passim; J. Wytzes, Der letzte Kampf des Heidentums,

Etudes préliminaires aux réligions orientales . . . , 56 (Leiden, 1977); recently, L. Cracco Ruggini, *Il paganesimo romano tra religione e politica*, Accademia Nazionale dei Lincei, Memorie, Classe scienze morali, storiche . . . ser. 8, 28, fasc. 1 (Rome, 1979). On the rebuilding of the monuments on the Forum, see Nash, *Dictionary*, 1:186ff (Basilica Julia); ibid., 2:294ff (Temple of Saturn; the date, whether early fourth century or later, as I believe, is still under debate); and ibid., 2:241ff (*porticus deorum consentium*). On the closing of the temples and the confiscation of the *fundi templorum*, in general, see Jerome, *Chronicle*, 233, ad. an. 331; *C Th*, XVI, 10. 3 (November 1, 346); ibid., XVI, 10. 4 (December 1, 354; closing); ibid., X, 1. 8 (February 4, 364; confiscation). The ineffectiveness of the first laws is evident from their repetition, notwithstanding the early destruction of individual temples in the East under Constantine (Eusebius, *VC* 3. 54–58 (Winkelmann, 107ff) and later, while in the West they were preserved as monuments of the past and state property. See, on this subject, F. W. Deichmann, "Frühchristliche Kirchen in antiken Heiligtümern," *JDAI* 54 (1939):105ff, and idem, "Die Basilika im Parthenon," *Athenische Mitteilungen* 63–64 (1938–39):127ff.

3 The origin, age, number, and function of the *tituli* before and after 313 remain in doubt: see Kirsch, *Titelkirchen*, passim, and more recently, Piétri, *Roma Christiana*, pp. 92ff. On the basilicas listed in our text, see *Corpus*, passim, and recent additions and corrections such as A. Prandi, *Il complesso . . . di SS. Giovanni e Paolo* (Vatican City, 1953); B. Apollonj-Ghetti, *S. Crisogono*, Le Chiese di Roma illustrate, 92 (Rome, 1966); H. Geertman, "Richerche sopra . . . S. Sisto Vecchio," *Rend Pont Accad* 41 (1968–69):219ff; D. Kinney, *S. Maria in Trastevere* . . . , Ph.D. thesis, New York University, 1975.

4 See Kinney, *S. Maria*, pp. 27ff, on the presumable obligation of popes to finance public buildings. On the *titulus Equitii*, see: *LP*, 1:17ff; Piétri, *Roma Christiana*, pp. 17ff; *Corpus*, 3:89, 121ff. For the *titulus Vestinae*, later dedicated to S. Vitale, see *LP*, 1:220ff, and *Corpus*, 4:313ff. For S. Sabina, see *LP*, 1:235, and *Corpus*, 4:72ff. For SS. Giovanni e Paolo, see *Corpus*, 1:270ff, and Prandi, *SS. Giovanni e Paolo*, who believes the basilica was built in Pammachius's lifetime. On the work of Leopardus and his committee—if that it was—see the inscriptions at S. Pudenziana (*Corpus*, 3:279ff) and S. Lorenzo fuori le Mura (*Corpus*, 2:8ff), the remarks in *LP*, 1:220 and 222, and, recently, Ch. Piétri, "Appendice prosopographique à *Roma Christiana* . . . ," *MEFRA* 89 (1977) 1:371ff, especially 377ff. On S. Pietro in Vincoli, see the inscriptions quoted in *Corpus*, 3:180ff, 229ff. On the formulae *hic fecit* and *hic dedicavit*, see H. Geertman, *More Veterum* (Groningen, 1975), pp. 190ff, perhaps overstating the exact meaning.

5 See *LP*, 1:172ff; R. McMullen, "Two Notes on Imperial Properties," *Athenaeum*, n.s. 54 (1976):19ff, especially 23, whence the quotation; Jones, *Later Roman Empire*, pp. 894ff; Piétri, *Roma Christiana*, pp. 79ff.

6 On the division of Church income into four parts, see Jones, *Later Roman*

Empire, pp. 894ff, referring to the letters of Simplicius (Ep. 1) and Gelasius (Ep. 14. 27) (A. Thiel, *Epistulae Romanorum pontificum genuinae* [Braunsberg, 1867], pp. 175ff, 378ff).

7 On the Augustan *regiones*, see H. Jordan, *Topographie der Stadt Rom in Altertum* (Berlin, 1878), 1. 1. 311ff. On the fourth century situation, the *regionaria*, see Valentini-Zucchetti, 1:63ff; on their interpretation, see L. Homo, *Rome Impériale . . .* (Paris, 1951), pp. 352ff. On the later development, see L. Duchesne, "Les régions de Rome au Moyen-Age," in *Scripta Minora* (Rome, 1973), pp. 91ff. It is worth noting that in the fifth century the old Augustan division, rather than that into seven ecclesiastical regions, appears to have obtained.

8 For the number of twenty-nine *tituli* in 499, see *MGH AA*, 12:405ff, as against twenty-four in 595, *Monumenta Germaniae Historica, Epistulae*, 1:366; see also Kirsch, *Titelkirchen*, pp. 7ff, and Piétri, *Roma Christiana*, pp. 92ff and 116ff, where the text suggests that the number of *domus ecclesiae* in the fourth century must have been far larger than those attested to by the official lists transmitted by the synods of 499 and 595 or summed up by the *Liber Pontificalis*; see, for instance, the *domus* where the presbyter Vitus celebrated Mass around 340 (Piétri, *Roma Christiana*, pp. 117ff).

9 On the problem of a renascence in late fourth- and fifth-century church design in Rome, see R. Krautheimer, "The Architecture of Sixtus III . . . ," in *De artibus opuscula XL . . . in Honor of Erwin Panofsky* (Princeton, 1961), pp. 191ff, and, with postscript, idem, *Studies*, pp. 181ff. Now I see the beginnings in the late fourth century more clearly even than at the time of writing that postscript. For a diametrically different view on the renascence problem, see F. W. Deichmann, *Die Spolien in der spätantiken Architektur*, Bayerische Akademie der Wissenschaften, Philosophisch-Historische Klasse, Sitzungberichte . . . , 1975–76 (Munich, 1975).

On the Romanization of foreign-born martyrs and the Princes of the Apostles as the true founders of Rome, see Piétri, "La Concordia Apostolorum . . . ," *MEFR* 63 (1961):275ff, and idem, *Roma Christiana*, pp. 1545ff, 1590ff. The Jerome quotation is from Ep. 127 (*Selected Letters of Saint Jerome*, LCL, 462).

10 On the pagan revival in Rome, see above, n. 2. On the foundation of S. Paolo fuori le Mura, see the imperial rescript, *Epistulae imperatorum pontificum . . .* (CSEL, 35, ed. O. Gunther), 46ff. On its dating, spring 384 or even late 383, see A. Chastagnol, "Quelques documents rélatifs à . . . Saint Paul hors-les-Murs," in *Mélanges . . . A. Piganiol*, 2 vols. (Paris, 1966), 1:421ff; also D. Vera, "Lo scandalo edilizio e . . . i titolari della 'praefectura urbis' dal 383 al 387 . . . ," *Studia et documenta historiae et iuris* 44 (1978):45ff, as against the date 386 maintained by L. M. Martinez y Fazio, *La segunda basilica de San Pablo . . ,* Miscellanea Historiae Pontificiae, 32 (Rome, 1872), pp. 209ff. On the foundation in the context of countering the late fourth-century pagan revival, see Krautheimer, "Intorno alla fondazione di S. Paolo f.l.m.," *Rend Pont Accad* 52 (1982), in press. The first approach to the emperors, suggesting foundation,

must antedate the rescript of 383–84 by some time, possibly as much as a year. Construction, on the other hand, can have started only after the date of the decree. On the building itself and its reconstruction in 441, see *Corpus*, 5:93ff.

11 On S. Maria Maggiore, see *Corpus*, 3:1ff; I am now convinced that the nave had a coffered ceiling, rather than an open timber roof. On Sto. Stefano Rotondo, see ibid., 4. 199ff; S. Corbett, "Santo Stefano Rotondo," *RAC* 35 (1960):229ff; and R. Krautheimer, "Success and Failure . . . ," in *Age of Spirituality: A Symposium*, ed. K. Weitzmann (New York, 1980), pp. 121ff. The linkage between Sto. Stefano and the Anastasis Rotunda postulated by me in 1935 ("Santo Stefano Rotondo a Roma e la Chiesa del Santo Sepolcro a Gerusalemme," *RAC* 12 [1935]:51ff) overshot the mark. The dependence of Sto. Stefano on its "model" in Jerusalem is more general than I then thought and is at best collateral. Our reconstruction of the interior is based on the fifteenth-century drawing in the Uffizi (Coll. Santarelli 161) attributed to Cronaca.

12 The population figures given in this paragraph are those provided by the *Enciclopedia Italiana* (Rome, 1900ff) 29:767ff, but they are sheer guesswork, and there is serious doubt whether by A.D. 400 Rome had more than half a million inhabitants, if that many.

On the mansions on the Celian and their abandonment, see Colini, *Celio*, passim; on that of the Valerii in particular, ibid., pp. 293ff, and G. Ferrari, *Early Roman Monasteries* (Vatican City, 1957), pp. 119ff; on the abandoned *tituli*, Kirsch, *Titelkirchen*, pp. 54ff. On the Esquiline markets, see F. Magi, *Il calendario dipinto sotto S. Maria Maggiore*, Atti Pont Accad, Memorie, 11, fasc. I (Vatican City, 1972), and Lugli, *Monumenti*, 3:418ff; on Roman housing, reused, B. M. Apollonj-Ghetti, *S. Prassede*, Le Chiese di Roma illustre, 66 (Rome 1961), especially figs. 4ff, and *Corpus*, 2:186ff, 3:283ff, and notes. The early third-century marble plan shows densely built-up areas on the Oppian (*Pianta marmorea*, pl. 18), the Tiber Island (ibid., pl. 30), and in the valley of the Passeggiata Archaeologica (ibid., pl. 15). Whether or not they were still fully occupied in the fifth century remains much in doubt, but in all likelihood they remained at least in part inhabited.

13 On baptism being conferred at Pentecost and, in case of urgency, at any time of the year, see Gelasius, Ep. 14. 10, dated 494 (A. Thiel, *Epistulae Romanorum pontificum genuinae*, pp. 368ff). J. Zettinger, "Die ältesten Nachrichten über Baptisterien der Stadt Rom," *RQSchr* 16 (1902):326ff, provides a reliable list of baptisteries documented in Rome prior to 500. On those at S. Crisogono and S. Marcello, see *Corpus*, 1:144ff, 2:211ff and 214ff, and B. M. Apollonj-Ghetti, *S. Crisogono*, pp. 24ff.

14 Station services without clergy at S. Agnese and elsewhere are mentioned in 366 "per cimiteria martyrum stationes sine clericis celebrabat, unde cum ad sanctam Agnem multi fidelium convenissent . . . ," (*Epistulae imperatorum pontificum . . .* , CSEL, 35:4ff). For liturgical stations at the martyrs' tombs as early as 336 and presumably before, see the calendar of 354, H. Lietzmann, *Die*

drei ältesten Martyrologien, Kleine Texte, 2 (Bonn, 1941), pp. 2ff, and C. L. Mohlberg, *Sacramentarium Veronense* (Rome, 1966), passim. For covered cemeteries and liturgical services at the grave, see Krautheimer, "Mensa—Coemeterium—Martyrium," *CA* 11 (1961): 1ff (also idem, *Studies*, pp. 35ff), and, in opposition, F. W. Deichmann, "Märtyrerbasilika, Martyrion, Memoria . . . ," *RM* 77 (1970): 144ff. On station services within the city in the fifth and sixth centuries, see the *Sacramentarium Veronense* (formerly called the *Leonianum*; the bulk of the prayers, according to Mohlberg, date between 450 and 550) and Th. Klauser, *Das römische Capitulare evangeliorum,* Liturgiegeschichtliche Quellen und Forschungen, 28 (Münster, 1935), passim (on p. xiii, Klauser suggests as a good possibility that the services go back to the fifth century). For the station services at the Lateran and St. Peter's in the fifth century (and perhaps earlier), see Piétri, *Roma Christiana,* pp. 112ff, 587ff, 590ff.

15 Hilarus's gift is listed in *LP*, 1:244ff: "In urbe vero Roma constituit ministeria qui circuirent constitutas stationes: scyphum aureum stationarium, pens. lib. VIII; scyphos argenteos xxv per titulos, pens. sing. lib. x; amas argenteas xxv, pens. sing. lib. x; calices argenteos ministeriales L, pens. sing. lib. II. Hic omnia in basilica Constantiniana uel ad sanctum Mariam constituta recondidit." See also Duchesne, ibid., 246ff, n. 9. For the station at S. Susanna, see Piétri, *Roma Christiana,* pp. 498ff.

16 For whatever it is worth in our fifth-century context, see the seventh-century list of twenty-six station churches inside the city, "istae vero ecclesiae intus Romae habentur . . . in his omnibus basilicis per certa tempora publica statio geritur," appended to the *De locis sanctis martyrum* (*Epitome Salisburgensis,* G. B. De Rossi, ed., *Roma Sotterranea,* 2 vols. [Rome, 1894], 1:143ff), while incomplete in that five church names are not filled in, counts only eight *tituli,* and these all by then provided with large church buildings, among the twenty-one churches named.

17 For the redecoration of the Lateran basilica in the fifth century, see *Corpus,* 5:10ff. For the apse, see ibid., pp. 428–30 (lost inscription). For the redecoration of the apse after 455, see *LP* 1:239ff. For the wall paintings in the nave, presumably also executed under Leo I, 440–61, like those at S. Paolo fuori le Mura and St. Peter's, see W. Köhler, ed., *Die karolingischen Miniaturen,* 4 vols. (Berlin, 1933ff), 1:2, 183ff, 206ff. For the baptistery, see G. B. Giovenale, *Il Battistero Lateranense* (Rome, 1929), superseded in part by G. Pelliconi, *Le nuove scoperte sulle origini del Battistero Lateranense,* Atti Pont Accad, Memorie, 12, fasc. 1 (Vatican City, 1975). Pelliconi's excavation has clarified the structures preceding the baptistery, but in my opinion he misinterprets the history of the building as it stands today. The basic mistake in Lafréri's reconstruction lies in his placing the springing of the ambulatory vault on the entablature of the lower, main order of columns instead of on that of the upper, minor order. Hence, the ambulatory would have been far higher. A study by R. Stapleford, *A Reconstruction of the Fifth Century Lateran Baptistery,* M. A. thesis, New York University, 1964, based on a survey prepared by Spencer Corbett and on a new

study and interpretation of the sixteenth-century drawings surviving, corrects Lafréri's reconstruction, but unfortunately remains unpublished.

18 On Hilarus's chapel of the Holy Cross and its atrium, see *LP*, 1:242f. Colini, *Celio*, pp. 369ff, lists most of the Renaissance surveys of the Oratory. See also *Corpus*, 5:93ff.

19 On St. Peter's, see *Corpus*, 5:165ff; on the Peutinger map, A. and M. Levi, *Itinera Picta* (Rome, 1967), pp. 169ff, and E. Weber, ed., *Tabula Peutingeriana*, 2 vols. (Graz, 1976), 1:segment 4.5.

20 The attribution, based on the wording *dedicavit*, of the planning of Sto. Stefano Rotondo to Simplicius's predecessor Hilarus is suggested by H. Geertman, *More Veterum* (Groningen, 1975), p. 190. For S. Bibiana, *Corpus*, 1:93ff, is super-seded by W. Buchowiecki, *Handbuch der Kirchen Roms* (Vienna, 1967), 1:468. The lists of clergy representing the title churches in 499 and 595 are found in: *MGH AA*, 12:405ff; ibid., Epp. 1. 366ff; also Kirsch, *Titelkirchen*, pp. 7ff.

21 For the (lost) mosaic at S. Maria Maggiore and its place in the apse, see G. A. Wellen, *Theotokos* (Utrecht, 1961); I am only too happy to withdraw the doubts regarding its placement published fifteen years ago (*Corpus*, 3:48ff). For Christmas service at the church, see C. Mohlberg, *Sacramentarium Veronense*, pp. 157ff, especially nos. 1244, 1245, 1270; see also Th. Klauser, *Das römische Capitulare evangeliorum*, p. 13 "in natale domini ad sanctam Mariam maiorem"; for Good Friday *ad Hierusalem*, see ibid., p. 23.

22 On the cross relic deposited by (or under) Constantine at S. Croce in Gerusa-lemme, see *LP*, 1:179ff and note 75. While A. Frolow, *La relique de la Vraie Croix* (Paris, 1962), pp. 177ff, is right in attributing the reference to the sixth-century compiler of the *LP*, it should be remembered that the church bore the epithet *Hierusalem* (and hence presumably sheltered a relic of the True Cross) by the second quarter of the fifth century, as witness a (lost) mosaic inscription set up by Galla Placidia, Valentinian III, and Honoria, and recorded in the *Sylloge Petri Sabini* (G. B. De Rossi, *Inscriptiones Christianae Urbis Romae septimo saeculo antiquiores* [Rome, 1888], 2. 1. 435ff; see also *Corpus*, 1:168ff). The designation of S. Croce in Gerusalemme as simply Hierusalem in *LP*, 1:179, is obviously inserted by the sixth-century compiler, as witness his expression, "usque in hodiernum diem." On the transfer of the relic from S. Croce in Gerusalemme to the Lateran by Hilarus, see *LP*, 1:242. For the eighth-century ritual at Rome, see De Rossi, *Inscriptiones Christianae Urbis Romae*, 2. 1. 34; for the fourth-century ritual at Jerusalem, see the report by Silvia Aetheria, in *Itinera Hierosolymitana*, ed. P. Geier (CSEL, 38) 88ff.

23 The Mass at S. Anastasia was introduced prior to Gregory I, but is not yet contained in the *Sacramentarium Veronense*; see also Piétri, *Roma Christiana*, pp. 590ff.

Index

Designer: Marilyn Perry
Compositor: G&S Typesetters
Printer: Malloy Lithographing
Binder: John H. Dekker
Text: 11/13 Sabon
Display: Sabon